Current
CONTROVERSIES

Nuclear Armament

Other Books in the Current Controversies Series

Nuclear Armament

Debra A. Miller, Book Editor

GREENHAVEN PRESS
A part of Gale, Cengage Learning

GALE
CENGAGE Learning

Detroit • New York • San Francisco • New Haven, Conn • Waterville, Maine • London

GALE
CENGAGE Learning™

Christine Nasso, *Publisher*
Elizabeth Des Chenes, *Managing Editor*

© 2011 Greenhaven Press, a part of Gale, Cengage Learning

Gale and Greenhaven Press are registered trademarks used herein under license.

For more information, contact:
Greenhaven Press
27500 Drake Rd.
Farmington Hills, MI 48331-3535
Or you can visit our Internet site at gale.cengage.com

For product information and technology assistance, contact us at

Gale Customer Support, 1-800-877-4253
For permission to use material from this text or product, submit all requests online at www.cengage.com/permissions

Further permissions questions can be emailed to permissionrequest@cengage.com

Articles in Greenhaven Press anthologies are often edited for length to meet page requirements. In addition, original titles of these works are changed to clearly present the main thesis and to explicitly indicate the author's opinion. Every effort is made to ensure that Greenhaven Press accurately reflects the original intent of the authors. Every effort has been made to trace the owners of copyrighted material.

Cover image copyright © Purestock/Alamy.

LIBRARY OF CONGRESS CATALOGING-IN-PUBLICATION DATA

Nuclear armament / Debra A. Miller, book editor.
    p. cm. -- (Current controversies)
  Includes bibliographical references and index.
  ISBN 978-0-7377-5630-2 (hbk.) -- ISBN 978-0-7377-5631-9 (pbk.)
  1. Nuclear weapons. 2. Nuclear weapons--Government policy. 3. National security. 4. Security, International. 5. Nuclear terrorism. 6. Ballistic missile defenses. 7. Nuclear weapons--Government policy--United States. I. Miller, Debra A.
  U264.N786 2011
  355.8'25119--dc22
                                    2011000875

Printed in the United States of America
1 2 3 4 5 6 7 15 14 13 12 11

Contents

The Pakistani Taliban poses a threat to the regime that governs Pakistan; there is also a risk that Taliban insurgents or al Qaeda terrorists could obtain nuclear material through attacks on Pakistan's vulnerable nuclear sites. Pakistan could reduce this risk by providing better protection for its nuclear arsenal but this would require greater cooperation with and assistance from the United States.

No: Nuclear Weapons Do Not Pose a Serious National Security Threat

Nuclear weapons have had very little military impact in the last sixty years; mostly they have just been a huge waste of money for both the United States and the Soviet Union. In the future, many countries will probably pursue nuclear disarmament voluntarily, and countries like Iran and North Korea will use nuclear weapons only as a deterrent. Furthermore, nuclear terrorism will not be a major threat, because it is very difficult to obtain, build, and detonate a nuclear bomb.

President Barack Obama wants to see a world free of nuclear weapons, but this would not necessarily make the world safer. US nonproliferation efforts have not prevented India, Pakistan, North Korea, or Iran from developing nuclear weapons, and if nuclear arms are outlawed, rogue nations will be the only ones with nuclear capability.

Chapter 2: Is There a Significant Threat of Nuclear Terrorism?

Yes: There Is a Significant Threat of Nuclear Terrorism

The United States and other countries are wisely trying to secure materials that could be used to make nuclear weapons because the threat of nuclear terrorism is a reality. Terrorist groups have the financial means to buy these materials and hire experts, and enriched uranium would be easy to transport and smuggle across national borders. Also, insurgents in Chechnya have already built and planted two dirty bombs, although neither was detonated.

President Barack Obama's administration has been emphasizing the dangers of nuclear terrorism; however, government experts say that there is no new intelligence information to support the claim that the terrorist nuclear threat is growing, and the latest CIA report suggests that this threat has diminished. The president's motivation may be political—part of the administration's push to eliminate nuclear weapons around the globe.

Chapter 3: Are Ballistic Missile Defense Systems Necessary?

The justification for a US missile defense system is that it would take a missile only thirty minutes to reach the United States from anywhere in the world. Furthermore, these missile threats are varied and rapidly evolving, as the number of nuclear nations grows and even more countries have ballistic missile capabilities. A comprehensive US missile defense system must be a priority.

It seems likely that the US missile defense system in Europe will be merged with the NATO missile defense system. However, a NATO missile shield will not work because countries with offensive missiles can easily produce countermeasures, and because the missile system produces geopolitical instability, since both Russia and China have small nuclear arsenals and would be threatened by the system. During these difficult economic times, this money could be better spent elsewhere.

Chapter 4: Is the US Response to the Nuclear Weapons Threat Adequate?

The 2010 Nuclear Posture Review is a comprehensive review of US nuclear strategy and policies. It can be expected to have a major impact in various areas, including the president's goal of reducing the number of nuclear weapons worldwide, the START negotiations with Russia, the nation's approach to the nuclear terrorism threat, and the actions to be taken to maintain or reduce US nuclear weapons arsenals and missile defense.

George Perkovich

The Barack Obama administration's new nuclear arms strategy released in April 2010 extends the US policy of trying to reduce the role and numbers of nuclear weapons. The new policy reflects reality; in any future war, the United States would use conventional not nuclear weapons, making nuclear weapons essentially irrelevant. The US military understands that nuclear weapons would only be used in one scenario—if a major nation launched a nuclear attack against the United States.

Stephen M. Walt

The new US nuclear policy announced by the Barack Obama administration states that the role of the US arsenal is to deter nuclear attacks; therefore, the United States will use nuclear weapons against nations that are not in compliance with the Nuclear Non-Proliferation Treaty. This basically means that the United States reserves the right to use nuclear weapons offensively against Iran and North Korea. This policy is mostly meaningless because the United States could always change its mind.

Charles Krauthammer

During the Cold War, the United States maintained an effective policy of nuclear deterrence that threatened nuclear retaliation against a Russian attack on Europe, even if Russia used conventional weapons. President Barack Obama's new nuclear policy weakens that posture and would not permit the United States to use nuclear power even if it is attacked with biological or chemical weapons, as long as the attacking country is in compliance with the Nuclear Non-Proliferation Treaty. This policy is naive and could encourage nuclear proliferation in countries that once relied on America's nuclear defense shield.

The Barack Obama administration's plan for ballistic missile defense proposes positive steps in some areas such as the Aegis system, but it also retreats in other areas such as the Airborne Laser system. With missile threats increasing from nations such as Iran and North Korea, this is the wrong time for the United States to tread water on missile defense. The United States needs a robust missile defense program.

Critics have assailed the Barack Obama administration's cancellation of plans for a Europe-based missile defense system, but this decision will not prevent the United States from defending against a missile attack. Rather, President Obama wisely shifted US missile defense in Europe to a ship-based antiballistic missile that can also be adapted to sites on land—a type of system that will be the most responsive to the type of threats the United States will be facing in the future.

Foreword

By definition, controversies are "discussions of questions in which opposing opinions clash" (Webster's Twentieth Century Dictionary Unabridged). Few would deny that controversies are a pervasive part of the human condition and exist on virtually every level of human enterprise. Controversies transpire between individuals and among groups, within nations and between nations. Controversies supply the grist necessary for progress by providing challenges and challengers to the status quo. They also create atmospheres where strife and warfare can flourish. A world without controversies would be a peaceful world; but it also would be, by and large, static and prosaic.

The Series' Purpose

The purpose of the Current Controversies series is to explore many of the social, political, and economic controversies dominating the national and international scenes today. Titles selected for inclusion in the series are highly focused and specific. For example, from the larger category of criminal justice, Current Controversies deals with specific topics such as police brutality, gun control, white collar crime, and others. The debates in Current Controversies also are presented in a useful, timeless fashion. Articles and book excerpts included in each title are selected if they contribute valuable, long-range ideas to the overall debate. And wherever possible, current information is enhanced with historical documents and other relevant materials. Thus, while individual titles are current in focus, every effort is made to ensure that they will not become quickly outdated. Books in the Current Controversies series will remain important resources for librarians, teachers, and students for many years.

In addition to keeping the titles focused and specific, great care is taken in the editorial format of each book in the series. Book introductions and chapter prefaces are offered to provide background material for readers. Chapters are organized around several key questions that are answered with diverse opinions representing all points on the political spectrum. Materials in each chapter include opinions in which authors clearly disagree as well as alternative opinions in which authors may agree on a broader issue but disagree on the possible solutions. In this way, the content of each volume in Current Controversies mirrors the mosaic of opinions encountered in society. Readers will quickly realize that there are many viable answers to these complex issues. By questioning each author's conclusions, students and casual readers can begin to develop the critical thinking skills so important to evaluating opinionated material.

Current Controversies is also ideal for controlled research. Each anthology in the series is composed of primary sources taken from a wide gamut of informational categories including periodicals, newspapers, books, US and foreign government documents, and the publications of private and public organizations. Readers will find factual support for reports, debates, and research papers covering all areas of important issues. In addition, an annotated table of contents, an index, a book and periodical bibliography, and a list of organizations to contact are included in each book to expedite further research.

Perhaps more than ever before in history, people are confronted with diverse and contradictory information. During the Persian Gulf War, for example, the public was not only treated to minute-to-minute coverage of the war, it was also inundated with critiques of the coverage and countless analyses of the factors motivating US involvement. Being able to sort through the plethora of opinions accompanying today's major issues, and to draw one's own conclusions, can be a complicated and frustrating struggle. It is the editors' hope that Current Controversies will help readers with this struggle.

Introduction

"Despite the horrific destruction caused by this first use of nuclear power, or perhaps because of it, many other nations sought to acquire their own nuclear weapons, leading to a worldwide nuclear arms race that continues to the present day."

Nuclear (also called atomic) weapons use the power of nuclear fission—energy derived from splitting apart atoms, the basic building blocks of matter—to produce massive explosions far more deadly than any other type of armament. German scientist and physicist Albert Einstein published the mathematical formula for the basic relationship between mass and energy ($E = mc^2$) in 1905, but it took several more decades of research to produce a sustainable nuclear fission reaction. Once this goal was attained, the early nuclear energy research focused on military applications—producing nuclear bombs that were used by the United States in 1945 against Japan to put an end to World War II. Despite the horrific destruction caused by this first use of nuclear power, or perhaps because of it, many other nations sought to acquire their own nuclear weapons, leading to a worldwide nuclear arms race that continues to the present day.

The Nuclear Age

The nuclear age began soon after Germany's aggressive actions against neighboring nations initiated World War II in Europe. In October 1939, Albert Einstein, who had fled from Germany to escape its authoritarian, anti-Jewish, and militaristic Nazi policies, sent a letter to US president Franklin D. Roosevelt, warning him that German leader Adolf Hitler wanted to develop a powerful bomb that would use a new source of energy—nuclear fission. Fearing that Germany could use such a weapon to rule the world, Roosevelt together with Great Britain launched a secret program to develop the nuclear weapon before Germany could do so. The program, code-named the Manhattan Project, was located in the United States, employed thousands of scientists and engineers, and was led by American physicist Robert Oppenheimer. Germany never was able to develop a nuclear bomb, and the Germans surrendered in May 1945; work on the Manhattan Project continued however because the war was still being fought against Germany's ally, Japan. The project achieved its first success on July 16, 1945, when scientists exploded a nuclear bomb test in the Alamogordo desert in New Mexico.

Just a month later, in August 1945, the United States became the first and only country to ever use nuclear arms against another nation. Despite Germany's surrender and after enduring heavy fire bomb attacks by British and American forces during the first half of 1945, Japan still refused to give up. This meant that the United States and its allies would have to begin a land invasion of Japan to end the war. Expecting that this planned invasion of Japan would cause massive casualties on both sides, US president Harry S. Truman instead decided to use the nuclear technology developed by the Manhattan Project to end the war. On August 6, US bombers dropped an atomic bomb on the Japanese city of Hiroshima. Days later, on August 9, when Japan still had not surrendered, a second bomb was used against the city of Nagasaki. Together, these bombs killed more than seventy thousand people instantly. In addition, many survivors suffered from heavy burns, radiation sickness, and related diseases such as leukemia and cancer—maladies that caused hundreds of thousands of more deaths by the end of 1945 and over the next five years. Most of those killed were civilians. Japan finally surrendered on August 15, 1945.

Nuclear Proliferation

After the war's end, the shock of the Hiroshima and Nagasaki bombings caused many people to call for a ban on nuclear weapons. However, the idea of giving up nuclear weapons soon ended as relations between the Soviet Union and the United States deteriorated, and the Soviets began a secret nuclear weapons program to catch up to the United States militarily. The Soviet program resulted in a successful testing on August 29, 1949. The United States, in turn, developed an even more advanced type of nuclear weapon, called the hydrogen bomb, or H-bomb. The H-bomb can produce an explosion one thousand times more powerful than the fission bombs used on Japan. This was the beginning of the Cold War—a fifty years arms race and period of tension between the two countries during which each side built up its nuclear and nonnuclear military forces.

The US-Soviet arms race led other countries to develop and test nuclear weapons. By 1961 both Britain and France became nuclear powers, and in 1964 China became the fifth country to possess nuclear weapons. This pattern of nuclear weapons proliferation caused many military and political experts to fear a worldwide spread of nuclear weapons. To prevent this scenario, the United States and the Soviet Union initiated international negotiations aimed at prohibiting the further spread of nuclear weapons. The result was the 1968 Treaty on the Non-Proliferation of Nuclear Weapons, also known as the Nuclear Non-Proliferation Treaty (NPT), which became effective March 5, 1970. Signatories to the NPT included the five countries then known to possess nuclear weapons (the United States, Soviet Union, United Kingdom, France, and China), plus fifty-nine other countries that did not have nuclear weapons that were known as the nonnuclear weapons nations. According to the provisions in the NPT, the nuclear weapons nations agreed not to release nuclear weapons or help other countries to acquire or build nuclear weapons, and to gradually reduce their nuclear arsenals, while the non-nuclear weapons nations agreed not to acquire or develop nuclear weapons. Since 1970, a number of other countries have signed the NPT as nonnuclear countries, bringing the total count of NPT countries to 189. The ultimate goal of the NPT is complete nuclear disarmament worldwide.

Some nonnuclear countries, however, refused to sign the NPT, believing it unfairly maintained a world order in which the five nuclear nations were the dominant powers. Also, over the years, certain nations that are not parties to the NPT have decided to defy the NPT and develop nuclear weapons programs in order to deter military aggression from other countries or enhance their global status. The first country to do this was India, which tested its first nuclear bomb in 1974. Thereafter, several other nations followed suit by pursuing nuclear research, including India's neighbor and political enemy Pakistan, as well as South Africa, Israel, Iraq, Iran, Libya, North Korea, and Syria. However, South Africa gave up its nuclear program and joined the NPT in 1991; Iraq's nuclear efforts were largely ended after the Persian Gulf War in the early 1990s and definitely terminated after the 2003 US-led invasion; and Libya voluntarily abandoned its nuclear weapons efforts in 2003. Also, in September 2007, Israel conducted an air strike that destroyed what it thought was a construction site of a nuclear research reactor in Syria, effectively ending that country's nuclear program.

Several other treaties relating to nuclear arms have also been negotiated, but like the NPT, they have not been completely successful. One is the Comprehensive Nuclear-Test-Ban Treaty (CTBT), a 1996 agreement that bans all testing of nuclear weapons. It has been signed and ratified by 153 nations but has not yet gone into effect. In addition, the United States and the Soviet Union have negotiated various agreements and treaties aimed at reducing nuclear arsenals. These have included the Strategic Arms Limitation Talks (SALT I and SALT II), the Vladivostok Agreement, the Intermediate-Range Nuclear Forces Treaty (INF), and the Strategic Arms Reduction Treaty (START).

Today's Nuclear Threats

Today, military experts believe that eight countries definitely possess nuclear weapons—five of them authorized nuclear nations under the terms of the NPT (the United States, Russia, Britain, France, and China), and three in defiance of the NPT (India, Israel, and Pakistan). In addition, experts believe that two other nations—North Korea and Iran—are continuing nuclear research and development with the goal of becoming nuclear powers. According to intelligence sources, North Korea already has the material to produce a small number of nuclear weapons and has conducted nuclear tests. Iran, meanwhile, is believed to be pursuing nuclear projects that could allow it to produce nuclear material and develop nuclear weapons within the next several years. The idea of North Korea and Iran having nuclear capability is particularly disturbing to US policy makers because both nations are considered to be rogue countries run by unstable and potentially aggressive regimes that might attack neighboring nations or even the United States itself. In addition, in the wake of the terrorist attacks on September 11, 2001, US policy makers have a new concern—the possibility that terrorist groups such as al Qaeda might obtain nuclear weapons and use them to threaten or attack the United States or other nations.

The issue of nuclear armament is the subject of the viewpoints contained in *Current Controversies: Nuclear Armament*. The authors present a range of views about whether nuclear weapons pose a serious national security threat, whether there is a significant threat of nuclear terrorism, whether ballistic missile systems are needed to protect the United States and its allies from nuclear attack, and whether the US government is responding appropriately to the nuclear threat.

CHAPTER 1

Do Nuclear Weapons Arsenals Pose a Serious National Security Threat?

Chapter Preface

Although the Soviet Union, led by Joseph Stalin, was a key ally of the United States during World War II, the two countries became bitter enemies and nuclear weapons rivals in the decades that followed the war's end. Although there were a couple of instances when military confrontation seemed likely, the United States and the Soviet Union never engaged militarily in a direct way. Instead, each country sought to extend its sphere of influence around the world through relationships with other countries while building up nuclear weapons and missile arsenals to fantastic levels. The ensuing arms race, which featured nuclear forces on both sides that could be deployed at a moment's notice, generated fear and tension for decades, roughly from 1945 to 1990—a period that became known as the Cold War. Eventually, however, the United States and the Soviet Union began negotiations to limit the spread of nuclear weapons and cut back on their own nuclear arsenals.

The US/Soviet relationship began to deteriorate following the Yalta Conference—a February 1945 meeting of the heads of government of the United States, the United Kingdom, and the Soviet Union (US president Franklin D. Roosevelt, British prime minister Winston Churchill, and Soviet Union general secretary Joseph Stalin) to discuss how Europe would be organized following the war. The Soviets, whose country had been invaded by Germany three times in the previous 150 years, made it clear that they wanted to establish a buffer zone on their western borders to prevent Germany from ever attacking again. To create this buffer, the Soviets wanted control over the countries located in this Eastern European region. Although the United States opposed this idea and pushed for self-determination in Eastern Europe, the Soviets ignored these concerns and proceeded to take control through military occupation. A few years later, in 1948, the Soviets also block-aded Germany's capital city of Berlin in an effort to control the entire city—an action that led the United States and Brit-ain to airlift food and supplies to city residents until 1949, when Germany was split into two nations—East Germany and West Germany. The United States and the Soviet Union again came close to hostilities after North Korea invaded South Ko-rea in 1950, purportedly with the knowledge and support of the Soviet Union and China. The result was the Korean War, fought by United Nations forces made up largely of American troops until the war ended in an uneasy armistice in 1953. A number of other near confrontations occurred in later years as Soviet-backed forces engaged with US-supported units in countries around the world. The most well-known example was the Vietnam War, a conflict in which the United States and the Soviet Union supported opposing factions in a war between North and South Vietnam.

The most defining feature of the Cold War, however, was the buildup of nuclear armaments. The Americans had devel-oped and used nuclear weapons in World War II, and the So-viet Union regarded the US possession of these weapons as a strategic threat. The Soviets therefore developed their own nuclear research program, exploding their first atomic bomb in 1948. When the United States responded by producing an even more powerful H-bomb, or hydrogen bomb, the Soviets countered by exploding one of their own. This arms race con-tinued throughout the 1950s, with the United States generally producing more nuclear weapons than the Soviet Union. The US military superiority was severely threatened in 1957, how-ever, when the Soviets launched Sputnik, the first successful satellite. Sputnik showed that the Soviets had the ability to reach American targets using space missiles—a technology for which the United States had no defenses. The United States, in turn, responded to Sputnik with its own space program, even-tually resulting in a successful moon landing in 1969.

By this time in the late 1960s, however, both the Soviet Union and the United States had enough nuclear weapons and missile delivery systems to destroy the entire world several times over. In addition, a number of other nations had entered the nuclear arms race and had developed or were researching nuclear weapons. Fear of further nuclear proliferation led the United States, the Soviet Union, the United Kingdom, and fifty-nine other countries to sign the Treaty on the Non-Proliferation of Nuclear Weapons, also known as the Nuclear Non-Proliferation Treaty (NPT), on July 1, 1968, in an effort to control the spread of nuclear armaments.

The pointlessness of continuing the nuclear arms race also led the United States and the Soviet Union to begin negotiations to limit the number of stockpiled nuclear weapons and missiles. The first effort in this direction began with talks between US president Richard M. Nixon and Soviet general secretary Leonid Brezhnev in 1969 known as the Strategic Arms Limitation Talks (SALT). SALT resulted in a historic arms limitations treaty that was signed in 1972, in which the United States and the Soviet Union agreed to peaceful coexistence, the avoidance of military confrontations, and no claims of spheres of influence. That same year, the two parties also signed the Anti-Ballistic Missile Treaty (ABM) to limit the number of antiballistic missile (ABM) systems used to defend areas against missile-delivered nuclear weapons. It was hoped that SALT would usher in a period of *détente*, a French word for the relaxation of tension, between the two nations. SALT, however, failed to end the Vietnam War, which was ongoing at this time, and the United States instead simply withdrew from the conflict in 1975. Furthermore, it did not prevent the Soviets from invading Afghanistan in 1979.

The failure of *détente*, and the election of US president Ronald Reagan in 1980, changed the US approach toward the Soviet Union. President Reagan implemented strong anticommunist policies that called for the United States to build up its military once again and to support anticommunist movements in places like Afghanistan. In 1982 President Reagan abandoned SALT and instead began a new set of nuclear reduction talks, known as the Strategic Arms Reduction Treaty (START) talks. Most important, however, in 1985 a new Soviet general secretary, Mikhail Gorbachev, came into power, heralding a complete change in Soviet military strategy and policies. Gorbachev introduced twin policies of *glasnost* (meaning openness) and *perestroika* (meaning economic restructuring), which effectively ended both the Soviets' military aggressiveness as well as its participation in the nuclear arms race. During Gorbachev's tenure, the Soviet Union's domination of Eastern Europe came to a close and the Berlin Wall, which had divided East and West Germany for decades, was torn down. In addition, in 1991, the two nations agreed to reduce their nuclear arsenals by about 30 percent. Signed on July 31, 1991, the START treaty limited each side to no more than six thousand nuclear warheads atop a total of sixteen hundred intercontinental ballistic missiles (ICBMs), submarine-launched ballistic missiles, and bombers. This treaty expired on December 5, 2009, but a new START treaty was signed in 2010 by US president Barack Obama and Russian president Dmitry Medvedev.

The end of the Cold War, according to some analysts, has substantially reduced the threat of nuclear weapons. Others disagree, arguing that there is still a nuclear threat from other nations that possess or are trying to build nuclear weapons, and that a new threat has emerged—nuclear terrorism. The viewpoints in this chapter debate this question of whether nuclear weapons arsenals continue to pose a national security threat for the United States.

There Is an Ongoing Danger of Nuclear War

Lawrence S. Wittner

Lawrence S. Wittner is a professor of history at the State University of New York at Albany, and he is the author of the book Confronting the Bomb: A Short History of the World Nuclear Disarmament Movement.

This August [2009], when hundreds of Hiroshima Day vigils and related antinuclear activities [special vigils and peace marches occur every August 6 to commemorate the dropping of the first atomic bomb] occur around the United States, many Americans will wonder at their relevance. After all, the nuclear danger that characterized the Cold War is now far behind us, isn't it?

Unfortunately, it is not.

Nuclear-Armed Nations

Today there are nine nuclear-armed nations, with over 23,000 nuclear weapons in their arsenals. Thousands of these weapons are on hair-trigger alert.

Admittedly, some nations are decreasing the size of their nuclear arsenals. The United States and Russia—which together possess about 95 percent of the world's nuclear weapons—plan to sign a treaty this year that will cut their number of strategic weapons significantly.

But other nations are engaged in a substantial nuclear buildup. India, for example, launched the first of its nuclear submarines this July and is also developing an assortment of land-based nuclear missiles. Meanwhile, Pakistan has been busy testing ballistic missiles and cruise missiles that will carry nuclear warheads, as well as constructing two new reactors to make plutonium for its expanding nuclear arsenal. Israel, too, is producing material for new nuclear weapons, while North Korea is threatening to resume its production.

In addition, numerous nations—among them, Iran—are suspected of working to develop a nuclear weapons capability.

But surely national governments are too civilized to actually *use* nuclear weapons, aren't they?

While nuclear weapons exist, there is a serious danger of accidental nuclear war.

In fact, one government (that of the United States) has already used atomic bombs to annihilate the populations of two cities.

Moreover, nations have come dangerously close to full-scale nuclear war on a number of occasions. The Cuban missile crisis [a confrontation between the Soviet Union, Cuba, and the United States] is the best-known example. But there are numerous others. In October 1973, during a war between Israel and Egypt that appeared to be spiraling out of control, the Soviet government sent a tough message to Washington suggesting joint—or, if necessary, Soviet—military action to bring the conflict to a halt. With President Richard Nixon reeling from the Watergate scandal . . . , his top national security advisors responded to what they considered a menacing Soviet move by ordering an alert of U.S. nuclear forces. Fortunately, cooler heads prevailed in the Kremlin, and the sudden confrontation eased short of nuclear war.

Of course, nuclear war hasn't occurred since 1945. But this fact has largely reflected public revulsion at the prospect and popular mobilization against it. Today, however, lulled by the end of the Cold War and the disintegration of the Soviet Union, we are in a period of relative public complacency. In this respect, at least, the situation has grown more dangerous.

Without countervailing pressure, governments find it difficult to resist the temptation to deploy their most powerful weapons when they go to war. And they go to war frequently.

A Danger of Accidental Nuclear War

Furthermore, while nuclear weapons exist, there is a serious danger of accidental nuclear war. In September 1983, the Soviet Union's launch-detection satellites reported that the U.S. government had fired its Minuteman intercontinental ballistic missiles, and that a nuclear attack on the Soviet Union was under way. Luckily, the officer in charge of the satellites concluded that they had malfunctioned and, on his own authority, prevented a Soviet nuclear alert. The incident was so fraught with anxiety that he suffered a nervous breakdown.

Another nuclear war nearly erupted two months later, when the United States and its NATO [North Atlantic Treaty Organization] allies conducted Able Archer 83, a nuclear training exercise that simulated a full-scale nuclear conflict, with NATO nuclear attacks upon Soviet nuclear targets. In the tense atmosphere of the time, recalled Oleg Gordievsky, a top KGB [the former Soviet Union's intelligence and internal security agency] official, his agency mistakenly "concluded that American forces had been placed on alert—and might even have begun the countdown to nuclear war." Terrified that the U.S. government was using this training exercise as a cover behind which it was launching a nuclear attack upon the Soviet Union, the Soviet government alerted its own nuclear forces, readying them for action. "The world did not quite reach the edge of the nuclear abyss," Gordievsky concluded. But it came "frighteningly close."

Nuclear Terrorism Dangers

Furthermore, today we can add the danger of nuclear terrorism. Although it is very unlikely that terrorists will be able to develop nuclear weapons on their own, the existence of tens of thousands of nuclear weapons and of the materials to build them in national arsenals opens the possibility that terrorists will acquire these items through theft or black market operations.

Overall, then, the situation remains very dangerous. Dr. Martin Hellman, a Professor Emeritus of Engineering at Stanford University who has devoted many years to calculating the prospects of nuclear catastrophe, estimates that the risk of a child born today suffering an early death through nuclear war is at least 10 percent. Moreover, he cautions that this is a conservative estimate, for he has not included the danger of nuclear terrorism in his calculations.

In June 2005, Senator Richard Lugar, then the Republican chair of the Senate Foreign Relations Committee, produced a committee report that was even less sanguine. Asked about the prospect of a nuclear attack within the next ten years, the 76 nuclear security experts he polled came up with an average probability of 29 percent. Four respondents estimated the risk at 100 percent, while only one estimated it at zero.

Thus, Hiroshima Day events provide a useful context for considering the ongoing nuclear danger and, conversely, the necessity for a nuclear weapons–free world.

The Dangers of Nuclear Weapons Are Greater than Ever Due to Proliferation and Terrorism

David Cortright

David Cortright is the director of policy studies at the Kroc Institute for International Peace Studies at the University of Notre Dame.

A few years ago, the notion of a world without nuclear weapons was merely an aspiration. Today it has become a widely accepted goal of international policy.

In September [2009], U.S. President Barack Obama presided over an extraordinary meeting of heads of state in the United Nations Security Council as it adopted Resolution 1887, resolving to "create the conditions for a world without nuclear weapons." Public officials and policy experts in numerous countries have taken up the call for disarmament that was issued three years ago by former U.S. national security officials George Shultz, Henry Kissinger, William Perry, and Sam Nunn.

In October 2009, the Kroc Institute for International Peace Studies and the Finnish Institute of International Affairs convened a meeting of policy makers and security experts in Helsinki, Finland, to deliberate on ways to strengthen the Nuclear Non-Proliferation Treaty [NPT, the Treaty on the Non-Proliferation of Nuclear Weapons], a cornerstone of the global effort to control nuclear weapons. Former U.S. Defense Secretary William Perry was a keynote speaker at the conference. Perry was part of the White House technical team in 1962 during the Cuban missile crisis [a confrontation between the United States, the Soviet Union, and Cuba].

The Real Risks

"We avoided nuclear war by luck, not by good management," he declared. Sixteen years later, while he was at the Pentagon, Perry was awakened at 3 a.m. by a call from a watch officer at the North American [Aerospace] Defense Command, warning of hundreds of incoming Soviet missile warheads (it proved to be a computer malfunction). "The risks of nuclear detonation are not theoretical," he said. "I experienced them firsthand."

Today the dangers of nuclear weapons are greater than ever, the result of proliferation and global terrorist threats. Nine countries have nuclear weapons. If North Korea and Iran acquire full nuclear weapons capability, the world may reach a proliferation tipping point, with the bomb spreading rapidly to other states. Pakistan has at least 50 nuclear weapons and is threatened by deepening internal instability and al Qaeda terrorists who have vowed to get their hands on the bomb. Traditional concepts of nuclear deterrence that apply to states have lost their meaning in a world of suicide bombers and non-state terrorist networks.

Global Cooperation

Overcoming these dangers will require unprecedented global cooperation to gain control over nuclear technologies and materials and to de-emphasize and ultimately eliminate reliance on nuclear weapons. The United States and Russia must lead the way. Together they possess 90 percent of the world's stockpile of more than 20,000 nuclear weapons. The two states are negotiating a new treaty that reduces nuclear weapons levels modestly and reinforces weapons monitoring and verification systems. Ratification of that treaty will be an urgent priority for the U.S. Senate in the months ahead.

The new strategic reduction treaty is a step in the right direction, but much deeper cuts will be needed in the future.

The United States and Russia also must work together to strengthen nonproliferation mechanisms and negotiate an international treaty to halt the production of fissile material. They should take weapons systems off hair-trigger alert and work with other governments to strengthen the authority and capacity of the International Atomic Energy Agency.

Especially important will be ratification of the Comprehensive [Nuclear-]Test-Ban Treaty, which makes permanent the existing moratorium on testing and outlaws nuclear explosions globally. Here again, U.S. Senate ratification will be essential. These and other good faith efforts by the major powers are necessary to win global cooperation for strengthened nonproliferation controls.

In May 2010, the 189 countries that are party to the Nuclear Non-Proliferation Treaty will gather at the United Nations in New York for an NPT five-year review conference, which is critically important for efforts to reduce the nuclear danger. Many leaders in the global South have long criticized the "do as I say not as I do" approach of the nuclear weapons states, which have been unwilling to negotiate for disarmament as required by Article VI of the NPT. Today the political climate is improving, thanks to the leadership of the United States and Britain, but the major powers must show concrete results to gain the global cooperation that is necessary to prevent further proliferation.

Achieving a world without nuclear weapons will take much time and effort, but the goal is now widely accepted as an essential requirement for international security. The way forward will require steady progress on steps toward the gradual reduction and elimination of nuclear weapons, coupled with continuous improvement in monitoring, verification, and international cooperation for peace and security.

There Is a Serious Threat That Pakistan's Nuclear Weapons Could Be Captured by Terrorists

Matthew Rojansky and Daniel Cassman

Matthew Rojansky is the deputy director of the Russia and Eurasia program at the Carnegie Endowment for International Peace. Daniel Cassman is a student at Stanford Law School.

Pakistani Taliban leader Baitullah Mehsud's death in August [2009] may have been a setback for militants in northwest Pakistan, but it was at best a temporary one. Decapitating the leadership of a militant organization is a notoriously poor way to address the grievances that feed extremism. Despite Mehsud's death, the threat of militants attacking or infiltrating Pakistan's nuclear program may be as great as ever. A recent report published by the Combating Terrorism Center at West Point in July revealed that in the past three years, terrorists have staged a series of dramatic attacks specifically targeting sensitive Pakistani nuclear facilities. In June, Afghan al Qaeda leader Mustafa Abu al-Yazid said the group would seek to capture Pakistani nuclear arms to use against America. With the will and ability of extremists to target Pakistan's most sensitive nuclear sites all but certain, the key questions are, how likely is it that these groups might actually get their hands on nuclear material, and how can that likelihood be decreased?

The Likelihood of Nuclear Terrorism

Expert assessments of whether Pakistani nuclear weapons or materials could fall into extremist hands vary widely, but most have been based on the same broad set of concerns about political instability and inadequate nuclear security. In a recent piece for *Arms Control Today*, Rolf Mowatt-Larssen, former head of the CIA's [Central Intelligence Agency's] terrorism efforts, cites the simultaneous growth of extremism, instability and the Pakistani nuclear arsenal itself as "worrying trends" that may compromise the army's ability to maintain control of its nuclear material. Even Woodrow Wilson [International] Center [for Scholars] fellow Feroz Hassan Khan, who argues that some Western fears about the safety of Pakistan's nuclear arsenal are exaggerated, admits that the theft of nuclear material is a valid concern.

Add the strong possibility of conflict with India over Kashmir to Pakistan's domestic risk factors and any crisis that threatened the state's control would leave the rest of the world worrying whether Pakistan's nuclear weapons had fallen into extremist hands. . . . Dr. Leonard Spector has argued that "once it was known that extremists had gained possession of the weapon-grade material, these groups could credibly claim to have a nuclear device." In effect, once nuclear material is known to have fallen outside Pakistani government control, the world might be held hostage to the demands of any terrorist group in the region.

Although Pakistan claims to have implemented some nuclear security measures based on American models, serious doubts remain about their efficacy.

So just how likely is any of this to occur? Though imaginable, the likelihood of various nightmare scenarios is impossible to predict because these scenarios depend on unknown or classified information. However, public data can shed light on the chances the extremists could successfully assault or infiltrate a specific nuclear facility, and on what they might find there.

Calculating the risk of such an assault requires several types of data, including the locations of materials (plutonium and highly enriched uranium), the areas under extremist control, and the areas most vulnerable to large-scale attack. . . .

The most threatened nuclear facilities are those at Chashma-Kundian, near Mianwali . . . , and the Wah Cantonment northwest of the capital, Islamabad. Chashma-Kundian is the site of two reactors and likely a reprocessing facility that produces weapons-grade plutonium. It is only about twenty kilometers from districts with a Taliban presence. Wah is less than sixty kilometers from Taliban-controlled areas, and is likely one of Pakistan's main nuclear weapons assembly facilities. An attack on any of those sites might net extremists enough nuclear material for a bomb—and Wah has already suffered multiple suicide bombings.

Pakistan's Nuclear Security Efforts

So how can these vulnerable sites be made more secure? Consider the valuable lessons from the Cooperative Threat Reduction (CTR) program, also known as Nunn-Lugar, under which the US and Russia dismantled thousands of nuclear warheads and secured tons of nuclear material at the end of the Cold War. Like Russia in the 1990s, Pakistan is a relatively poor country with a fragile political system, located in an unstable region. To address these risks, CTR provided expertise and funding to upgrade security at nuclear facilities, including better screening of personnel. Over the longer term, the program set up better tracking and protection for nuclear materials in transit, and ways to transition ex-weapons scientists into lucrative, peaceful research. CTR shows that greatly enhanced security is possible, assuming high levels of trust and strict verification between officials and experts on both sides. Achieving that level of cooperation with Pakistan will be very difficult.

Although Pakistan claims to have implemented some nuclear security measures based on American models, serious doubts remain about their efficacy. Experience from CTR suggests that the government's commitment to a security blueprint is worth little without consistent monitoring and improvement of security measures on the ground. Unfortunately, Pakistan has proven unwilling to accept more intrusive American help or advice on nuclear security since US assistance embarrasses the government and stokes popular paranoia about Westerners seeking to control the country's nuclear arsenal. And Pakistan has refused to accept any help if doing so will compromise the locations of its nuclear weapons or facilities, perpetuating a tenuous balance between secrecy and vulnerability.

Without more active US help, Pakistan's nuclear facilities will remain unacceptably vulnerable to terrorist assault or infiltration.

To improve nuclear security through CTR-type cooperation, the US should seek to improve the overall relationship with Pakistan. Civilian casualties in ongoing US drone strikes against Taliban and al Qaeda forces are a major source of anger in Pakistan and must be minimized. But the central challenge is to move beyond the US-India-Pakistan strategic triangle. To start, the US must persuade Islamabad that the Islamic militants, whom Pakistan has tacitly supported as a thorn in India's side, are themselves the greatest threat to Pakistan's national security. Given the risk of extremists compromising Pakistan's nuclear program, the US, India and Pakistan share a basic interest in combating both terrorism and proliferation.

Cooperation against this shared threat must begin with steps by Pakistan to dismantle Lashkar-e-Taiba, the group responsible for last year's three-day terror assault in Mumbai, and now a symbol to many Indians of Pakistan's ill will. A concerted US effort to reopen talks on Kashmir could also build trust by fulfilling what Pakistanis believe was an Obama campaign promise, while lowering tensions with India. Obama envoy Richard Holbrooke has so far refused to broach the Kashmir issue because of the strong Indian objection to a US role. But without publicizing such talks, the US should find ways to promote dialogue between the two countries.

Without more active US help, Pakistan's nuclear facilities will remain unacceptably vulnerable to terrorist assault or infiltration, particularly in key locations where a growing nuclear program and the ongoing, widespread Islamist insurgency intersect. Although the Pakistani Taliban may be momentarily weakened, the broader risk to Pakistan's nuclear arsenal remains. Real "cooperative threat reduction" in Pakistan must place greater emphasis on cooperation, trust-building, and a broader regional security dialogue that includes India.

Nuclear Weapons Are Not as Dangerous as World Leaders Claim

John Mueller

John Mueller is a professor of political science at Ohio State University and author of the book Atomic Obsession: Nuclear Alarmism from Hiroshima to Al Qaeda.

N*uclear Weapons Are the Greatest Threat to Humankind.* No. But you might think so if you listen to world leaders right now. In his first address to the U.N. [United Nations] Security Council, U.S. President Barack Obama warned apocalyptically, "Just one nuclear weapon exploded in a city—be it New York or Moscow, Tokyo or Beijing, London or Paris—could kill hundreds of thousands of people. And it would badly destabilize our security, our economies, and our very way of life." Obama has put nuclear disarmament back on the table in a way it hasn't been for decades by vowing to pursue a nuclear-free world, and, with a handful of big treaty negotiations in the works, he seems to think 2010 has become a critical year.

But the conversation is based on false assumptions. Nuclear weapons certainly are the most destructive devices ever made, as Obama often reminds us, and everyone from peaceniks to neocons seems to agree. But for more than 60 years now all they've done is gather dust while propagandists and alarmists exaggerate their likelihood of exploding—it was a certainty one would go off in 10 years, [physicist and novelist] C.P. Snow authoritatively proclaimed in 1960—and nuclear metaphysicians spin fancy theories about how they might be deployed and targeted.

Nuclear weapons have had a tremendous influence on the world's agonies and obsessions, inspiring desperate rhetoric, extravagant theorizing, and frenetic diplomatic posturing. However, they have had very limited actual impact, at least since World War II. Even the most ingenious military thinkers have had difficulty coming up with realistic ways nukes could conceivably be applied on the battlefield; moral considerations aside, it is rare to find a target that can't be struck just as well by conventional weapons. Indeed, their chief "use" was to deter the Soviet Union from instituting [Adolf] Hitler-style military aggression, a chimera [imaginary monster] considering that historical evidence shows the Soviets never had genuine interest in doing anything of the sort. In other words, there was nothing to deter.

Instead, nukes have done nothing in particular, and have done that very well. They have, however, succeeded in being a colossal waste of money—an authoritative 1998 Brookings Institution study showed the United States had spent $5.5 trillion on nukes since 1940, more than on any program other than Social Security. The expense was even more ludicrous in the cash-starved Soviet Union.

Nuclear weapons are already disappearing, and elaborate international plans like the one Obama is pushing aren't needed to make it happen.

And that does not include the substantial loss entailed in requiring legions of talented nuclear scientists, engineers, and technicians to devote their careers to developing and servicing weapons that have proved to have been significantly unnecessary and essentially irrelevant. In fact, the only useful part of the expenditure has been on devices, protocols, and policies to keep the bombs from going off, expenditures that would, of course, not be necessary if they didn't exist.

Evaluating Obama's Plan to Eliminate Nuclear Weapons

Obama's Plan to Eliminate Nuclear Weapons Is a Good One. Not necessarily. Obama's plan, unveiled before the world in a speech in Prague last April [2010], represents an ambitious attempt to rid the world of nukes. Under the president's scheme, developing countries would have access to an internationally monitored bank of nuclear fuel but would be barred from producing weapons-grade materials themselves. Existing warheads would be secured and major powers such as Russia and the United States would pledge to scale back their weapons programs. In September, the U.N. General Assembly passed a resolution in support of Obama's proposal, giving his massive project some institutional backing.

But all of this is scarcely needed. Nuclear weapons are already disappearing, and elaborate international plans like the one Obama is pushing aren't needed to make it happen. During the Cold War, painstakingly negotiated treaties did little to advance the cause of disarmament—and some efforts, such as the 1972 SALT [Strategic Arms Limitation Talks] agreement, made the situation worse from a military standpoint. With the easing of tensions after the Cold War, a sort of negative arms race has taken place, and the weapons have been going away more or less by themselves as policy makers wake up to the fact that having fewer useless things is cheaper than having more of them. By 2002, the number of deployed warheads in Russian and U.S. arsenals had dropped from 70,000 to around 30,000, and it now stands at less than 10,000. "Real arms control," wistfully reflected former U.S. assistant secretary of state for arms control Avis Bohlen in an essay last May [2009], "became possible only when it was no longer necessary."

Indeed, both sides have long found that arms reductions were made more difficult if they were accomplished through explicit mutual agreements requiring that an exquisitely nuanced arrangement be worked out for every abandoned nut and bolt. In 1991, for example, the Americans announced that they were unilaterally reducing tactical nuclear weapons, and the Soviet Union soon followed, a development hailed by a close observer, Brown University scholar Nina Tannenwald, as "the most radical move to date to reverse the arms race" and a "dramatic move away from 'war fighting' nuclear postures." This "radical" and "dramatic" feat was accomplished entirely without formal agreement. For the most part, the formal arms-control process has been left trying to catch up with reality. When the U.S. Senate in 1992 ratified a nuclear arms reduction treaty, both sides had already moved to reduce their weapons even further than required by that agreement.

France has also unilaterally cut its arsenal very substantially—though explaining why France needs any nukes is surely a *problématique* worthy of several impenetrable dissertations. (Perhaps to threaten former colonies that might otherwise abandon French for English?) The British, too, are under domestic political pressure to cut their nuclear arsenal as they wrestle with how many of their aging nuclear subs they need to hang on to (how about: none?), and the Chinese have built far fewer of the weapons than they could have—they currently stock just 180.

A negative arms race is likely to be as chaotic, halting, ambiguous, self-interested, and potentially reversible as a positive one. However, history suggests that arms reduction will happen best if arms negotiators keep out of the way. Formal disarmament agreements of the kind Obama seeks are likely simply to slow and clutter the process.

But all nukes are not likely to vanish entirely, no matter the method. Humanity invented these weapons, and there will still be nuclear metaphysicians around, spinning dark, improbable, and spooky theoretical scenarios to justify their existence.

A Nuclear Explosion and the U.S. Economy

Nuclear Explosion Would Cripple the U.S. Economy. Only if Americans let it. Although former CIA [Central Intelligence Agency] chief George Tenet insists in his memoirs that one "mushroom cloud" would "destroy our economy," he never bothers to explain how the instant and tragic destruction of three square miles somewhere in the United States would lead inexorably to national economic annihilation. A nuclear explosion in, say, New York City—as Obama so darkly invoked—would obviously be a tremendous calamity that would roil markets and cause great economic hardship, but would it extinguish the rest of the country? Would farmers cease plowing? Would manufacturers close their assembly lines? Would all businesses, governmental structures, and community groups evaporate?

It turns out that getting one's hands on a working nuclear bomb is actually very difficult.

Americans are highly unlikely to react to an atomic explosion, however disastrous, by immolating themselves and their economy. In 1945, Japan weathered not only two nuclear attacks but intense nationwide conventional bombing; the horrific experience did not destroy Japan as a society or even as an economy. Nor has persistent, albeit nonnuclear, terrorism in Israel caused that state to disappear—or to abandon democracy.

Even the notion that an act of nuclear terrorism would cause the American people to lose confidence in the government is belied by the traumatic experience of Sept. 11, 2001 [9/11, terrorist attacks on the United States], when expressed confidence in America's leaders paradoxically soared. And it contradicts decades of disaster research that documents how socially responsible behavior increases under such conditions—seen yet again in the response of those evacuating the World Trade Center on 9/11.

Russia's Loose Nuclear Arsenal

Terrorists Could Snap Up Russia's Loose Nukes. That's a myth. It has been soberly, and repeatedly, restated by Harvard University's Graham Allison and others that Osama bin Laden gave a group of Chechens $30 million in cash and two tons of opium in exchange for 20 nuclear warheads. Then there is the "report" about how al Qaeda acquired a Russian-made suitcase nuclear bomb from central Asian sources that had a serial number of 9999 and could be exploded by mobile phone.

If these attention-grabbing rumors were true, one might think the terrorist group (or its supposed Chechen suppliers) would have tried to set off one of those things by now or that al Qaeda would have left some trace of the weapons behind in Afghanistan after it made its very rushed exit in 2001. Instead, nada. It turns out that getting one's hands on a working nuclear bomb is actually very difficult.

In 1998, a peak year for loose nuke stories, the head of the U.S. Strategic Command made several visits to Russian military bases and pointedly reported, "I want to put to bed this concern that there are loose nukes in Russia. My observations are that the Russians are indeed very serious about security." Physicists Richard Garwin and Georges Charpak have reported, however, that this forceful firsthand testimony failed to persuade the intelligence community "perhaps because it [had] access to varied sources of information." A decade later, with no credible reports of purloined Russian weapons, it rather looks like it was the general, not the spooks, who had it right.

By all reports, Russian nukes have become even more secure in recent years. It is scarcely rocket science to conclude that any nuke stolen in Russia is far more likely to go off in

Red Square than in Times Square. The Russians seem to have had no difficulty grasping this fundamental reality.

Setting off a stolen nuke might be nearly impossible anyway, outside of TV's *24* and disaster movies. Finished bombs are routinely outfitted with devices that will trigger a nonnuclear explosion to destroy the bomb if it is tampered with. And, as Stephen Younger, former head of nuclear weapons research and development at Los Alamos National Laboratory, stresses, only a few people in the world know how to cause an unauthorized detonation of a nuclear weapon. Even weapons designers and maintenance personnel do not know the multiple steps necessary. In addition, some countries, including Pakistan, store their weapons disassembled, with the pieces in separate secure vaults.

Al Qaeda's Interest in Nuclear Weapons

Al Qaeda Is Searching for a Nuclear Capability. Prove it. Al Qaeda may have had some interest in atomic weapons and other weapons of mass destruction (WMD). For instance, a man who defected from al Qaeda after he was caught stealing $110,000 from the organization—"a lovable rogue," "fixated on money," who "likes to please," as one FBI [Federal Bureau of Investigation] debriefer described Jamal al-Fadl—has testified that members tried to purchase uranium in the mid-1990s, though they were scammed and purchased bogus material. There are also reports that bin Laden had "academic" discussions about WMD in 2001 with Pakistani nuclear scientists who did not actually know how to build a bomb.

But the Afghanistan invasion seems to have cut any schemes off at the knees. As analyst Anne Stenersen notes, evidence from an al Qaeda computer left behind in Afghanistan when the group beat a hasty retreat indicates that only some $2,000 to $4,000 was earmarked for WMD research, and that was mainly for very crude work on chemical weapons. For comparison, she points out that the Japanese millennial terrorist group, Aum Shinrikyo, appears to have invested $30 million in its sarin gas manufacturing program. Milton Leitenberg of the Center for International and Security Studies [at Maryland] at the University of Maryland-College Park quotes Ayman al-Zawahiri as saying that the project was "wasted time and effort."

Even former International Atomic Energy Agency inspector David Albright, who is more impressed with the evidence found in Afghanistan, concludes that any al Qaeda atomic efforts were "seriously disrupted"—indeed, "nipped in the bud"—by the 2001 invasion of Afghanistan and that after the invasion the "chance of al Qaeda detonating a nuclear explosive appears on reflection to be low."

Making a Nuclear Bomb Is Not Easy

Fabricating a Bomb Is Child's Play. Hardly. An editorialist in *Nature*, the esteemed scientific journal, did apply that characterization to the manufacture of uranium bombs, as opposed to plutonium bombs, last January, but even that seems an absurd exaggeration. Younger, the former Los Alamos research director, has expressed his amazement at how "self-declared 'nuclear weapons experts,' many of whom have never seen a real nuclear weapon," continue to "hold forth on how easy it is to make a functioning nuclear explosive." Uranium is "exceptionally difficult to machine," he points out, and "plutonium is one of the most complex metals ever discovered, a material whose basic properties are sensitive to exactly how it is processed." Special technology is required, and even the simplest weapons require precise tolerances. Information on the general idea for building a bomb is available online, but none of it, Younger says, is detailed enough to "enable the confident assembly of a real nuclear explosive."

A failure to appreciate the costs and difficulties of a nuclear program has led to massive overestimations of the ability to fabricate nuclear weapons. As the 2005 Silberman-Robb commission, set up to investigate the intelligence failures that led to the Iraq war, pointed out, it is "a fundamental analytical error" to equate "procurement activity with weapons system capability." That is, "simply because a state can buy the parts does not mean it can put them together and make them work."

Iran will most likely "use" any nuclear capability in the same way all other nuclear states have: for prestige (or ego-stoking) and deterrence.

For example, after three decades of labor and well over $100 million in expenditures, Libya was unable to make any progress whatsoever toward an atomic bomb. Indeed, much of the country's nuclear material, surrendered after it abandoned its program, was still in the original boxes.

Iranian and North Korea's Interest in Nukes

Iranian and North Korean Nukes Are Intolerable. Not unless we overreact. North Korea has been questing after nuclear capability for decades and has now managed to conduct a couple of nuclear tests that seem to have been mere fizzles. It has also launched a few missiles that have hit their presumed target, the Pacific Ocean, with deadly accuracy. It could do far more damage in the area with its artillery.

If the Iranians do break their solemn pledge not to develop nuclear weapons (perhaps in the event of an Israeli or U.S. air strike on their facilities), they will surely find, like all other countries in our nuclear era, that the development has been a waste of time (it took Pakistan 28 years) and effort (is Pakistan, with its enduring paranoia about India and a growing jihadi threat, any safer today?).

Moreover, Iran will most likely "use" any nuclear capability in the same way all other nuclear states have: for prestige (or ego-stoking) and deterrence. Indeed, as strategist and Nobel laureate Thomas Schelling suggests, deterrence is about the only value the weapons might have for Iran. Such devices, he points out, "should be too precious to give away or to sell" and "too precious to 'waste' killing people" when they could make other countries "hesitant to consider military action."

If a nuclear Iran brandishes its weapons to intimidate others or get its way, it will likely find that those threatened, rather than capitulating or rushing off to build a compensating arsenal, will ally with others (including conceivably Israel) to stand up to the intimidation. The popular notion that nuclear weapons furnish a country with the ability to "dominate" its area has little or no historical support—in the main, nuclear threats over the last 60 years have either been ignored or met with countervailing opposition, not with timorous acquiescence. It was conventional military might—grunts and tanks, not nukes—that earned the United States and the Soviet Union their respective spheres of influence during the Cold War.

In his 2008 campaign, Obama pointedly pledged that, as president, he would "do everything in my power to prevent Iran from obtaining a nuclear weapon . . . everything." Let us hope not: The anti-proliferation sanctions imposed on Iraq in the 1990s probably led to more deaths than the bombs dropped on Hiroshima and Nagasaki, and the same can be said for the ongoing war in Iraq, sold as an effort to root out Saddam Hussein's nukes. There is nothing inherently wrong with making nonproliferation a high priority, so long as it is topped with a somewhat higher one: avoiding policies that can lead to the deaths of tens or hundreds of thousands of people under the obsessive sway of worst-case-scenario fantasies.

Obama has achieved much in his first year as president on foreign policy through toning down rhetoric, encouraging openness toward international consultation and cooperation, and helping revise America's image as a threatening and arrogant loose cannon. That's certainly something to build on in year two.

The forging of nuclear arms reduction agreements, particularly with the Russians, could continue the process. Although these are mostly feel-good efforts that might actually hamper the natural pace of nuclear arms reductions, there is something to be said for feeling good. Reducing weapons that have little or no value may not be terribly substantive, but it is one of those nice gestures that can have positive atmospheric consequences—and one that can appear to justify certain Nobel awards.

The confrontations with Iran and North Korea over their prospective or actual nukes are more problematic. Obama and Secretary of State Hillary Clinton have already contributed big time to the hysteria that has become common coin within the foreign-policy establishment on this issue. It is fine to apply diplomacy and bribery in an effort to dissuade those countries from pursuing nuclear weapons programs: We'd be doing them a favor, in fact. But, though it may be heresy to say so, the world can live with a nuclear Iran or North Korea, as it has lived now for 45 years with a nuclear China, a country once viewed as the ultimate rogue. If push eventually comes to shove in these areas, the solution will be a familiar one: to establish orderly deterrent and containment strategies and avoid the temptation to lash out mindlessly at phantom threats.

Eliminating Nuclear Weapons Will Not Make the World Safer

Washington Times

The Washington Times *is a daily newspaper published in Washington, D.C.*

When it comes to the nuclear-weapons issue, President [Barack] Obama wants to be a global community organizer. However, what we really need are some tough beat cops with a mandate to clean up the neighborhood.

A World Without Nuclear Weapons

On Thursday [September 24, 2009], the United Nations Security Council unanimously adopted a resolution drafted by the United States that calls upon, urges, encourages, but does not require U.N. member states to take various actions to curb the proliferation of nuclear weapons. Mr. Obama chaired the meeting and pressed the vision of a nuclear-weapons-free world that he had introduced in April. In the practical world of counterproliferation, the president is making little progress in dissuading Iran from building nuclear weapons, has rewarded serial proliferator North Korea with bilateral negotiations and is silent on Venezuela's announced intention to start a nuclear program.

The president's "no nukes" stance makes a nice bumper sticker, but achieving it will take more than feel-good rhetoric. French President Nicolas Sarkozy objected to the fact that the Security Council resolution did not mention Iran and North Korea, currently the two greatest problem states. "We live in a real world," Mr. Sarkozy said, "not a virtual world." But Mr. Obama said he did not want to single out any particular country. After all, we might offend them. It says something when France demonstrates a stronger international leadership role than the United States and well illustrates the style-over-substance approach of the Obama administration. Mr. Sarkozy wants results; Mr. Obama seeks applause.

Nuclear Arms and Strategic Interests

The premise that a nuclear-weapons-free world would be safer is highly questionable. In the right hands, nuclear weapons play an important deterrence role. The problem is that they increasingly are being obtained by countries ruled by left-wing dictators and other unsavory types who either cannot be deterred or do not want to be. These bad actors understand that they can harness deterrence to their benefit. The United States is unlikely to risk concerted action against a country with a demonstrated nuclear-weapons capability and nothing to lose. Countries such as Iran and Venezuela see North Korea as a positive inspiration—an extremely poor country with about the same per capita gross domestic product as Chad but treated as a major player in world affairs primarily because of its atomic program. We shudder to imagine how much more powerful Tehran [the capital of Iran] or Caracas [the capital of Venezuela] would be with the same capabilities.

If nuclear arms are outlawed, only outlaws will have nuclear arms.

Self-interest points toward proliferation, not away from it, and formal arms control of the type the president advocates has a dubious record when stacked against strategic interests. The Strategic Arms Limitation [Talks] (SALT) agreements between the United States and Soviet Union codified massive increases in what already were the largest nuclear arsenals in human history. But since the end of the Cold War, the total number of warheads between the two countries has declined 90 percent—not because of arms-control treaties but as the natural consequence of reduced tensions after the collapse of communism. Meanwhile, since the Nuclear Non-Proliferation Treaty [the Treaty on the Non-Proliferation of Nuclear Weapons] took effect four decades ago, India, Pakistan and North Korea have tested nuclear weapons; Israel is widely believed to possess them; and the Iranian bomb is right around the corner.

The United States is showing itself unwilling to take the hard steps necessary to stop nuclear proliferation. Countries that are willing to defy the international community know they can have the bomb if they make the investment and are patient. They might have to ride out some international sanctions, but once they have conducted a nuclear test and joined the club, they will have all the leverage they need.

Last week, Mr. Obama lectured the world that "international law is not an empty promise"—but laws that are not enforced become exactly that. If nuclear arms are outlawed, only outlaws will have nuclear arms.

Current
CONTROVERSIES

CHAPTER 2

Is There a Significant Threat of Nuclear Terrorism?

Chapter Preface

The world's main effort to control nuclear weapons over the last forty years has been the Treaty on the Non-Proliferation of Nuclear Weapons, also known as the Nuclear Non-Proliferation Treaty (NPT)—a landmark international treaty negotiated in 1968 to prevent the spread of nuclear weapons and weapons technology, to promote the peaceful uses of nuclear energy, and to further the goal of worldwide nuclear disarmament. The NPT has now been signed and ratified by 189 nations, including the five nations that possessed nuclear weapons at the time the agreement was negotiated (the United States, the Soviet Union, the United Kingdom, France, and China) as well as scores of nonnuclear countries. The treaty is enforced by the International Atomic Energy Agency (IAEA), an international agency created by the United Nations. The IAEA is responsible for policing the nuclear activities of countries to make sure that they pursue peaceful nuclear activities and that they do not produce nuclear weapons.

The origins of the NPT can be found in a plan proposed by US president Harry S. Truman at the end of World War II, when the United States was the only country in the world that possessed nuclear weapons. In a proposal called the Baruch Plan, President Truman offered to destroy the US nuclear arsenal if other countries would agree not to acquire nuclear weapons and would permit inspections to verify that agreement. Under Truman's plan, an agency under the jurisdiction of the United Nations Security Council would have been given the sole authority over nuclear weapons research and the power to conduct inspections to make sure nations were not developing nuclear weapons. The Soviet Union rejected this idea; it was already in the process of developing nuclear weapons capability. The US Congress therefore enacted the 1946 US Atomic Energy Act to ban the release of nuclear technology to other countries.

With the failure of Truman's nonproliferation plan, the next US president, Dwight Eisenhower, pursued a different strategy. President Eisenhower's 1953 Atoms for Peace program sought to provide assistance to other countries to help them develop nuclear energy for peaceful purposes. The IAEA was created at this time to assist with this process. The program allowed the United States, the Soviet Union, and other countries to provide information, research reactors, and small amounts of nuclear fuel (highly enriched uranium) to nonnuclear nations around the world.

As peaceful nuclear technology spread, however, many people began to worry that it could be put to use to build nuclear weapons. In 1962, the United States proposed a draft treaty to the Soviet Union to prevent countries with nuclear weapons from transferring them or the weapons technology to nonnuclear weapons countries. In addition, the United States proposed that countries without nuclear weapons should agree not to acquire or manufacture them in the future. The Soviets initially balked at this idea, largely because of concerns about the US commitments to its allies to deploy nuclear weapons in places such as Germany, a historic Soviet enemy close to the Soviet Union's western border. Also, before the negotiations had ended, two other nations had become nuclear weapons powers—France and China. The final treaty, the Nuclear Non-Proliferation Treaty, basically banned all signing members except five—the United Kingdom, China, France, the Soviet Union, and the United States—from having nuclear weapons and committed those five nations to eventually eliminating their atomic arsenals. The IAEA was given the authority to conduct inspections of nuclear facilities to ensure that these conditions were met. The NPT became effective in 1970, and over the years it was signed and ratified by numerous countries. Two countries, India and Israel, who participated in the NPT negotiations and who did not yet have nuclear weapons capability, refused to join because they wanted the option to acquire nuclear weapons in the future. In 1995, the NPT was extended indefinitely beyond its initial twenty-five-year term.

Many analysts have praised the NPT for its success in preventing a rapid proliferation of nuclear weapons over the decades it has been in force, but some countries have defied its ban on nuclear weapons activities. India conducted its first nuclear weapons test in 1974—a development that inspired its neighbor, Pakistan, to accelerate its own nuclear weapons research. Pakistan claims it acquired the ability to explode a nuclear bomb in 1987. Israel is widely believed to have acquired nuclear weapons capability no later than the early 1970s. Libya, too, was conducting nuclear research, but eventually abandoned this effort. In recent years, intelligence information has revealed that Iraq, North Korea, and Iran have hid nuclear weapons research activities from IAEA inspectors. Iraq's nuclear program ended with the 2003 American-led invasion, but North Korea conducted a successful nuclear weapons test in 2006. Current debate surrounds Iran's nuclear activities. Although most experts say that Iran does not yet have the ability to make nuclear bombs, the IAEA has discovered that Iran conducted various types of nuclear research in secret, suggesting that the goal is to produce nuclear weapons. Today, there are a total of eight nations known or widely believed to possess nuclear weapons and the missiles to deliver them—the original five authorized in the NPT plus India, Israel, and Pakistan. Two others, Iran and North Korea, appear to be getting close to becoming nuclear weapons powers.

Despite these NPT failures, analysts suggest that without the NPT, there could easily be as many as thirty countries with nuclear weapons by now. They credit the NPT with establishing a clear global goal of nonproliferation, increasing the taboo against nuclear weapons, and providing incentives for countries to remain free of nuclear weapons. Still other nuclear experts suggest that the biggest danger from nuclear weapons today is not governments, but rather the possibility that nuclear weapons could end up in the hands of nongovernmental groups—specifically terrorist groups such as al Qaeda—which might have few inhibitions about deploying them. This chapter addresses the issue of whether there is a significant danger from nuclear terrorism.

The Threat of Nuclear Terrorism Is Real

Jennifer Hesterman

Jennifer Hesterman is a professor at the American Military University as well as an author, lecturer, and analyst on military warfare and terrorism.

The United States again reasserted itself as the world's police last week [April 12, 2010], leading the way to secure thousands of pounds of fissile materials that could be used to build nuclear weapons such as dirty bombs. Countries around the world have agreed to identify, secure and convert this material before it falls into the hands of criminal gangs that would gladly sell to the highest bidder.

The Danger of Nuclear Terrorism

Point #1—Do not underestimate the sophistication of a terrorist group. We've routinely done that as a nation, and the consequences were deadly on 9/11 [referring to the terrorist attacks on the United States on September 11, 2001]. Al Qaeda could certainly have the right people on the "payroll"—scientists, engineers, technical experts—infused with the radical Islamist ideology and ready to help the cause.

Point #2—Do not underestimate the finances of terrorist groups. Many are engaged in narco-trafficking, where millions of dollars trade hands daily.

Point #3—Despite the best detection efforts at airports and in major cities, highly enriched uranium could easily be transported and smuggled. Expert Graham Allison (author of *Nuclear Terrorism: The Ultimate Preventable Catastrophe*) says it takes only about 35 pounds . . . of highly enriched uranium to make a nuclear bomb. This amount of material is easily transportable and could be smuggled along established trafficking routes by highly paid "mules."

We have already expended billions chasing "suitcase" nukes, which are said to exist, are missing, and are possibly in the hands of al Qaeda.

Point #4—On the subject of dirty bombs—the materials needed, like medical isotopes, might be pretty easily obtained, and it is true they alone would not yield much radiation. The main issue with a dirty bomb would be the blast itself . . . unless some relatively high-grade uranium was employed. Then a dirty bomb would not only have immediate, but long-lasting radiation effects at the point of detonation.

Point #5—We've already seen a dirty bomb built by terrorists and "employable," in fact it happened over 15 years ago. In 1995, a conventional bomb containing radioactive cesium was found in Izmailovsky Park in Moscow, planted by Chechen rebels. They planted a similar bomb again in 1998. Both times, the rebels alerted law enforcement and the weapon was not detonated. However, they achieved one of the main goals of terrorism—causing fear among the populace.

The bottom line is the terrorists only need to threaten to use a nuclear weapon to heighten fear and panic among Americans. We have already expended billions chasing "suitcase" nukes, which are said to exist, are missing, and are possibly in the hands of al Qaeda. We still don't have a definitive answer, but the enemy forced us down that path, which naturally we must follow since it is a fight we can't afford to lose.

Or terrorists could detonate a conventional weapon or IED [improvised explosive device], then send a tape to news media stating it was a nuclear weapon. The panicked reaction from our uneducated populace (our fault by keeping them in the dark) would be overwhelming and it would take days for the government to convince citizens there was no nuclear material involved in the blast. Depending on where this event occurred, for instance Wall Street, the resulting economic damage could be grave.

Educating the Public

We have a problem with the American public that our government has unwillingly created. First of all, there is an overreliance by the public on law enforcement, the military and first responders to take care of them—as witnessed in the hurricane events a few years back. These agencies are resource constrained and would be unable to fully take care of the public in the event of a nuclear emergency, but admitting this would be a sign of weakness. Next, we have not fully educated the public on the threat which is present and looms larger than ever because these are not nation-state actors, these are asymmetric actors with apocalyptic agendas.

Finally, we have not educated the public on how to take care of themselves, family, work colleagues, etc., during and after the event. Actually, we Americans know less now about the nuclear threat and related facts than previous generations! Remember the bomb shelter signs on buildings? People keeping water, canned food, can openers, radios with batteries, etc., in a safe place at home that would serve as a shelter for the family? Even though this is our profession, we are probably all guilty of not being fully prepared ourselves.

Studies have proven that a person who is educated before a crisis is less fearful. Armed with knowledge, they feel more in control. They can DO something, not just wait for help. I am reminded of the man who was trapped in the rubble in the hotel in Haiti with a severe leg injury. He had recently downloaded a first aid application on his iPod and while trapped, he used that information to treat his injury and not bleed to death, or go into shock. It probably also increased his confidence, will to live and to find a way to get himself out of the situation, not just wait for help. And die waiting.

I hope Americans were listening last week when our president and many other heads of state articulated the nuclear threat by terrorists, but I sincerely doubt it. We should have followed up this news with a huge DHS [Department of Homeland Security]-led education campaign on nuclear weapons—what they are, the effects, how to prepare and what to do in the event of an attack. Why are we afraid to have this frank discussion with our citizens? We can all do our part by continuing to spread the facts about this threat and educate (arm) our colleagues, families and friends.

Nuclear Terrorism Is One of the Greatest Threats to Global Security

Barack Obama

Barack Obama is a former US senator who was elected the forty-fourth president of the United States in 2008.

It is my privilege to welcome you to Washington and to formally convene this historic summit [the Nuclear Security Summit, which convened on April 12, 2010]. We represent 47 nations from every region of the world, and I thank each of you for being here. This is an unprecedented gathering to address an unprecedented threat.

The Risk of Nuclear Terrorism

Two decades after the end of the Cold War, we face a cruel irony of history—the risk of a nuclear confrontation between nations has gone down, but the risk of nuclear attack has gone up.

Nuclear materials that could be sold or stolen and fashioned into a nuclear weapon exist in dozens of nations. Just the smallest amount of plutonium—about the size of an apple—could kill and injure hundreds of thousands of innocent people. Terrorist networks such as al Qaeda have tried to acquire the material for a nuclear weapon, and if they ever succeeded, they would surely use it. Were they to do so, it would be a catastrophe for the world—causing extraordinary loss of life, and striking a major blow to global peace and stability.

In short, it is increasingly clear that the danger of nuclear terrorism is one of the greatest threats to global security—to our collective security.

Barack Obama, "Obama's Speech at the Nuclear Security Summit," Council on Foreign Relations, April 13, 2010. www.cfr.org. Reproduced by permission.

And that's why, one year ago today in—one year ago in Prague, I called for a new international effort to secure all vulnerable nuclear materials around the world in four years. This is one part of a broader, comprehensive agenda that the United States is pursuing—including reducing our nuclear arsenal and stopping the spread of nuclear weapons—an agenda that will bring us closer to our ultimate goal of a world without nuclear weapons.

Over the past year, we've made progress. At the United Nations Security Council last fall, we unanimously passed Resolution 1887 endorsing this comprehensive agenda, including the goal of securing all nuclear materials. Last night, in closed session, I believe we made further progress, pursuing a shared understanding of the grave threat to our people.

An Opportunity for Progress

And today, we have the opportunity to take the next steps.

We have the opportunity, as individual nations, to take specific and concrete actions to secure the nuclear materials in our countries and to prevent illicit trafficking and smuggling. That will be our focus this morning.

We have the opportunity to strengthen the International Atomic Energy Agency, the IAEA, with the resources and authorities it needs to meet its responsibilities. That will be our focus at our working lunch.

We have the opportunity, as an international community, to deepen our cooperation and to strengthen the institutions and partnerships that help prevent nuclear materials from ever falling into the hands of terrorists. And that will be our focus this afternoon.

And we have the opportunity, as partners, to ensure that our progress is not a fleeting moment, but part of a serious and sustained effort. And that's why I am so pleased to announce that President Lee [Myung-bak] has agreed to host the next Nuclear Security Summit in the Republic of Korea in two years. This reflects South Korea's leadership, regionally and globally, and I thank President Lee and the South Korean people for their willingness to accept this responsibility. . . .

So today is an opportunity—not simply to talk, but to act. Not simply to make pledges, but to make real progress on the security of our people. All this, in turn, requires something else, which is something more fundamental. It will require a new mind-set—that we summon the will, as nations and as partners, to do what this moment in history demands.

I believe strongly that the problems of the 21st century cannot be solved by any one nation acting in isolation. They must be solved by all of us coming together.

At the dawn of the nuclear age that he helped to unleash, Albert Einstein said: "Now everything has changed. . . ." And he warned: "We are drifting towards a catastrophe beyond comparison. We shall require a substantially new manner of thinking if mankind is to survive."

That truth endures today. For the sake of our common security, for the sake of our survival, we cannot drift. We need a new manner of thinking—and action. That is the challenge before us. And I thank all of you for being here to confront that challenge together, in partnership.

The United States Is Inviting Nuclear Terrorism Because of Its Unsecured Border with Mexico

Norah Petersen

Norah Petersen is a journalist and frequent contributor to American Thinker, *a daily Internet publication that emphasizes national security and other issues of importance to Americans.*

According to Bob Woodward's forthcoming book *Obama's Wars*, the United States is not prepared for a nuclear terrorist attack:

A "potential game-changer" for us or for our enemies? What exactly does the president mean? On the topic of nuclear terrorism, economist and prolific author Thomas Sowell warned in 2009:

> "It took only two nuclear bombs to get Japan to surrender—and the Japanese of that era were far tougher than most Americans today. Just one bomb—dropped on New York, Chicago or Los Angeles—might be enough to get us to surrender."

Sowell's fears of a nuclear attack from Iran were at the forefront of his warning; yet, another continual threat which cannot be decoupled from the risk of nuclear terrorism is the crisis of our virtually unguarded border with Mexico. In 2004, *Time* magazine reported:

> "Sharif al-Masri, an Egyptian who was captured in late August near Pakistan's border with Iran and Afghanistan, has told his interrogators of 'al-Qaeda's interest in moving

nuclear materials from Europe to either the U.S. or Mexico,' according to a report circulating among U.S. government officials. Masri also said al-Qaeda has considered plans to 'smuggle nuclear materials to Mexico, then operatives would carry materials into the U.S.'"

It is now believed that terrorist at large, Adnan el-Shukrijumah, may have traveled into the United States via the Mexican border during 2004. A *Wall Street Journal* op-ed by Representative Jane Harman and Senator Susan Collins related that Shukrijumah is "a trained nuclear technician allegedly tasked by al Qaeda with carrying off an 'American Hiroshima.'" The op-ed further stated that Shukrijumah "once sought radioactive material from a university in Ontario, Canada" and that "news reports allege that this was an attempt to construct a dirty bomb."

Unfortunately, despite the danger of nuclear terrorism, little has changed over the years regarding border security, or lack thereof. In August [2010], *Investor's Business Daily* reported that illegal immigrants from terrorist-sponsoring countries continually enter the United States through the Mexican border:

> "In the last three years, the Department of Homeland Security caught and released 481 illegal aliens from nations designated as state sponsors of terrorism and 'countries of interest,' and those 481 are now fugitives. That may seem like a small number out of the thousands that arrive every day, but it took only 19 terrorists to fly passenger jets into the World Trade Center, the Pentagon and target the White House or Congress.

> After a Nigerian passenger dubbed the Christmas Day bomber almost succeeded in blowing up Northwest [Airlines] Flight 253 near Detroit, Nigeria and 13 other countries were put on a list whereby passengers from these countries flying into the U.S. would be subject to extra scrutiny and screening.

Ten of these countries—Afghanistan, Algeria, Iraq, Lebanon, Libya, Nigeria, Pakistan, Saudi Arabia, Somalia and Yemen—were defined as 'countries of interest.' Four others—Cuba, Iran, Sudan and Syria—are listed as state sponsors of terror. Yet citizens from these countries routinely walk across or are brought across our southern border."

Not only are we "woefully unprepared" for a nuclear attack, we are inexcusably allowing conditions which greatly increase the possibility of one.

The Threat of Nuclear Terrorism Is Exaggerated

Bill Gertz and Eli Lake

Bill Gertz is geopolitics editor and a national security and investigative reporter for the Washington Times *newspaper. He also is the author of six books. Eli Lake is a national security correspondent for the* Washington Times.

T he [Barack] Obama administration is warning that the danger of a terrorist attack with nuclear weapons is increasing, but U.S. officials say the claim is not based on new intelligence and questioned whether the threat is being overstated.

President Obama said in a speech before the 47-nation Nuclear Security Summit, which concluded Tuesday [April 13, 2010], that "the risk of a nuclear confrontation between nations has gone down, but the risk of nuclear attack has gone up."

The two-day meeting concluded with an agreement by participants to take steps to prevent non-state actors like al Qaeda from obtaining nuclear weapons, either through theft of existing weapons or through making their own with pilfered nuclear material.

The joint statement called nuclear terrorism one of the most challenging threats to international security and called for tougher security to prevent terrorists, criminals and others from acquiring nuclear goods.

A Lack of Intelligence on the Nuclear-Terrorism Threat

But Henry Sokolski, a member of the congressional Commission on the Prevention of Weapons of Mass Destruction Pro-

Bill Gertz and Eli Lake, "Critics: Obama Admin Hyping Terrorist Nuclear Risk," washingtontimes.com, April 14, 2010. Copyright © 2010 by The Washington Times. All rights reserved. Reproduced by permission.

liferation and Terrorism, said that there is no specific intelligence on ongoing terrorist procurement of nuclear material.

"We were given briefings and when we tried to find specific intelligence on the threat of any known terrorist efforts to get a bomb, the answer was we did not have any."

Mr. Obama told reporters that there was a range of views on the danger but that all the conferees "agreed on the urgency and seriousness of the threat."

Mr. Sokolski said the idea that "we know that this is eminent has got to be somehow informed conjecture and apprehension, [but] it is not driven by any specific intelligence per se."

The administration appears to be inflating the danger ... hyping intelligence to support its policies.

"We have reasons to believe this and to be worried, but we don't have specific intelligence about terrorist efforts to get the bomb," he said. "So we have to do general efforts to guard against this possibility, like securing the material everywhere."

A senior U.S. intelligence official also dismissed the administration's assertion that the threat of nuclear terrorism is growing.

"The threat has been there," the official said. "But there is no new intelligence."

The official said the administration appears to be inflating the danger in ways similar to what critics of the [George W.] Bush administration charged with regard to Iraq: hyping intelligence to support its policies.

The Goal: Nuclear Disarmament

The official said one likely motivation for the administration's new emphasis on preventing nuclear terrorism is to further the president's goal of eliminating nuclear weapons. While the U.S. nuclear arsenal would be useful in retaliating against a sovereign state, it would be less so against a terrorist group. But if the latter is the world's major nuclear threat, the official explained, then the U.S. giving up its weapons seems less risky.

The administration recently signed an agreement with Russia that would cut U.S. nuclear weapons and delivery systems to 1,550 warheads and 800 delivery vehicles. During the Cold War, the U.S. and Soviet nuclear arsenals both topped 10,000 warheads.

Mr. Obama said during a news conference that the summit was part of a larger effort to "pursue the peace and security of a world without nuclear weapons."

Sen. Jon Kyl, Arizona Republican, said he was disappointed that the summit did not do more to focus on Iran.

The nonbinding communiqué issued during the summit "largely restates current policy, and makes no meaningful progress in dealing with nuclear terrorism threats or the ticking clock represented by Iran's nuclear weapons program," Mr. Kyl said in a statement.

A Diminishing Threat of Nuclear Terrorism?

The new focus on nuclear terrorism emerged recently in the Nuclear Posture Review report made public last week that identified nuclear terrorism as "today's most immediate and extreme danger."

By contrast, the latest CIA [Central Intelligence Agency] report to Congress on arms proliferation suggested that the threat from nuclear terrorism had diminished. It stated that several terrorist groups, including al Qaeda, "probably remain interested" in chemical, biological, radiological and nuclear arms "but not necessarily in all four of those capabilities."

Additionally, the report, made public last month, said terrorists "aim to use these agents against Western targets, especially in Iraq and Afghanistan."

The military's blueprint for future conflicts, "Joint Operating Environment 2010," stated that terrorists obtaining nuclear weapons or other mass-destruction arms is a "possibility" and said a major worry is that extremists could seize power in Pakistan and gain access to its nuclear arsenal.

The Joint Forces Command report warned that devastating biological weapons attacks by nations or terrorist groups could produce "terror on the scale of a nuclear attack."

John Brennan, the White House's chief counterterrorism adviser, told reporters Monday that the threat of nuclear terrorism "is real, it is serious, it is growing, and it constitutes one of the greatest threats to our national security and, indeed, to global security."

A National Security Council spokesman declined to provide further information on Mr. Brennan's or the president's statement that the nuclear terrorist threat is growing.

Mr. Brennan said al Qaeda has sought a nuclear weapon for the past 15 years and that its efforts continue today.

Al Qaeda is seeking "highly enriched uranium or separated plutonium" for a weapon that would give the Islamist group "the ability not only to threaten our security and world order in an unprecedented manner, but also to kill and injure many thousands of innocent men, women and children, which is al Qaeda's sole agenda," Mr. Brennan said.

Al Qaeda's efforts to obtain nuclear weapons in the past have included reports that the group tried to purchase a stolen weapon in the former Soviet Union, and that it has worked with Pakistani nuclear scientists.

Former CIA director George Tenet disclosed in his recent memoir that a Pakistani nongovernmental organization, Umma Tameer-e-Nau, was used as cover for a covert program to send Pakistani nuclear scientists to work with al Qaeda's nuclear weapons team when it was granted safe haven in Afghanistan before 2001.

However, Brian [Michael] Jenkins, author of the book *Will Terrorists Go Nuclear?* and a RAND Corp. adviser, said that al Qaeda in the past has been duped by supposed nuclear suppliers who initiated scams that suggest a "naivete and lack of technical capability on the part of the organization," he said.

"We have evidence of terrorist ambitions to obtain nuclear weapons or nuclear material but we have no evidence of terrorist capabilities to do either," he said.

In late 2001, after the U.S. invaded Afghanistan in the wake of the Sept. 11 terrorist attacks, some materials were discovered in al Qaeda bases such as crude diagrams of the basic components of a nuclear bomb.

Mr. Jenkins, however, said that U.S. technical specialists concluded from the designs that al Qaeda did not have the ability to produce a nuclear weapon.

In 2002, members of al Qaeda's affiliate in Saudi Arabia attempted to purchase Russian nuclear devices through al Qaeda's leadership in Iran, though the transactions did not move forward.

In his 2007 memoir, *At the Center of the Storm*, Mr. Tenet wrote that "from the end of 2002 to the spring of 2003, we received a stream of reliable reporting that the senior al Qaeda leadership in Saudi Arabia was negotiating for the purchase of three Russian nuclear devices."

Graham Allison, a Harvard professor and author of a book on nuclear terrorism, said he agrees with the president that the threat is growing, based on North Korea's nuclear proliferation to Syria and instability in nuclear-armed Pakistan.

"What's new is a willingness to put the spotlight on this issue and say, 'This is the face of nuclear danger today,'" he said.

The Nuclear Terrorist Threat Is Not as Significant as World Leaders Say

Alex Wilner

Alex Wilner is a fellow with the Macdonald-Laurier Institute, a Canadian public policy group, and he is a senior researcher at the ETH, a science and technology university in Zurich, Switzerland.

One of my favourite movies is *The Sum of All Fears*, the 2002 blockbuster adaptation of Tom Clancy's 1991 best-selling novel.

The plot centers on a nuclear strike on the city of Baltimore orchestrated by an international, neo-Nazi terrorist organization with aspirations of sparking a Russian-American war to facilitate the rise of a German empire. The arch bad guy, Austrian neo-Nazi Richard Dressler, purchases the device on the black market and smuggles it into the US by cargo ship. The bomb, concealed in a pop machine, is picked up and delivered to its target (the Baltimore football stadium) by an American member of Dressler's group. It detonates during a football game with the American president in attendance. Post-detonation, it's up to American academic/CIA [Central Intelligence Agency] analyst/millionaire stockbroker/future American president and all-round wunderkind, Jack Ryan, to unravel the terrorist plot and diffuse global tensions. SPOILER ALERT! The nuclear device is an American product constructed in the 1960s and secretly delivered to Israel to assist its nascent nuclear program. The bomb is lost when the Israeli jet carrying it is shot down over Syria during the Yom Kippur War (1973) and is buried in the desert until it is unearthed and sold by the arms trader decades later.

The Nuclear Security Summit

This past week [April 12–13, 2010], President [Barack] Obama convened the first Nuclear Security Summit in Washington, D.C., with a script pulled right out of Clancy's book.

Delegates from nearly 50 countries met to discuss the threat of nuclear terrorism. Obama's goal was to persuade them to agree on steps that would deny terrorists the materials needed for nuclear attacks (plutonium and/or highly enriched uranium). He called for better protection of nuclear materials within each country and greater multilateral capacity to control nuclear materials globally. Canada did its part by urging others to support its 2002 initiative (the Global Partnership Program) to secure nuclear sites in the former USSR [Union of Soviet Socialist Republics—the former Soviet Union], by agreeing to safeguard and curb its use of weapons-grade uranium in its national research reactors, and by calling on other states to phase out the use of highly enriched uranium in their own research initiatives.

These are all worthy policy goals and deserve our full attention. But reading the news coverage, official transcripts, editorials, and analysis of the summit, you would be excused if you considered the threat of a nuclear "catastrophe" higher today than during the Cold War, if you believed the acquisition of nuclear materials by terrorists was an effortless task, and accepted with near certainty that nuclear terrorism was just around the proverbial corner.

It isn't that nuclear terrorism isn't a grave concern or that the summit didn't produce some good; it's just that the nuclear hyperbole flowing from Washington was a little thick.

For instance, Obama's opening remarks included these warnings:

- "Nuclear materials that could be sold or stolen and fashioned into a nuclear weapon exist in dozens of nations."

- "Just the smallest amount of plutonium—about the size of an apple—could kill and injure hundreds of thousands of innocent people."

- "Terrorist networks such as al Qaeda have tried to acquire the material for a nuclear weapon, and if they ever succeeded, they would surely use it."

- "We are drifting towards a catastrophe beyond comparison. We shall require a substantially new manner of thinking if mankind is to survive."

Others followed suit.

The odds that al Qaeda ... will have the dollars, industrial infrastructure, scientific know-how, resolve, and time to develop their own nukes approaches zero.

In the *New York Times*, former IAEA [International Atomic Energy Agency] Director General Mohamed ElBaradei, Harvard Professor Graham Allison, and former Mexican President Ernesto Zedillo called nuclear terrorism "the biggest potential threat to civilization" adding that "the highly enriched uranium required to make an elementary nuclear bomb could be hidden inside a football." And Robert Gallucci, a former US nuclear proliferation negotiator, was quoted in the *Globe and Mail* suggesting that "it is possible, plausible and ... probable that a ... terrorist group will set off a nuclear blast." It's just a matter of time, really, before terror goes nuclear.

But where's the nuance? With all the squawking going on in Washington the rest of us missed out on the few critical points of contention that should help inform policy.

Terrorists Cannot Develop Their Own Nuclear Weapons

Over a period of 60 years, only a handful of states have managed to autonomously develop nuclear weapons. The odds that al Qaeda or another non-state organization will have the dollars, industrial infrastructure, scientific know-how, resolve, and time to develop their own nukes approaches zero. [Author] Brian Michael Jenkins suggests in *Will Terrorists Go Nuclear?* that it isn't impossible that terrorists may build nuclear weapons, but it isn't very likely either. There's evidence that Osama bin Laden has sought nuclear weapons, but Jenkins presents al Qaeda's quest as "naïve, poorly informed, and vulnerable to con artists." Obama knows this, which is why the recent summit focused on bulking up security of existing nuclear materials (which makes it harder for terrorists to steal what they may want) and strengthening global counterterrorism norms, institutions, and conventions (which further dissuades the very few states who might think about sharing WMD [weapons of mass destruction] know-how with non-state actors).

States Are Not Likely to Share Their Nuclear Arsenals with Terrorists

While it is true that some regimes certainly do support international and regional terrorism, sponsoring nuclear terrorism is of a totally different order of magnitude. No state has much to gain by doing so. Concerning Iran, the current patron of terror, [security expert] Daniel Byman writes that it is "not likely [to] transfer chemical, biological, or nuclear weapons to terrorist groups," because doing so "offers Iran few tactical advantages," Tehran has grown "more cautious in its backing of terrorists" since 9/11 [September 11, 2001, terrorist attacks on the United States], and it is "highly aware" that supporting nuclear terrorism would incur unprecedented "U.S. wrath and international condemnation." Simply put, supporting a WMD terrorist attack is the surest way to regime change and doesn't make rational sense.

Buying a Nuclear Weapon Isn't That Easy

The best thing about black markets is that they can be destabilized and destroyed. The weakest point in a black market system, [foreign affairs professor] Thomas Schelling explained at a recent conference in Zurich [Switzerland], is the relationship between a seller and a buyer: each has to trust that the other will produce the goods to be exchanged. One way states can disrupt this system and make it harder for peddlers and purchasers of nuclear material is to actively introduce uncertainty into the buyer-seller relationship. For instance, the US might consider clandestinely entering the nuclear black market as either a buyer or a seller. As a buyer, it can locate those individuals and groups selling materials, track them down and/or eliminate them, or buy the material and destroy it. As a seller, the US can make contact with potential buyers, trade them shoddy goods, and/or capture and eliminate them. By doing both, the US disrupts the market forces, adds uncertainty to the process, and destabilizes the system. The end result is that neither the terrorist nor the criminal would know who to trust.

Nuclear Possession Might Not Necessarily Lead to Nuclear Use

The assumption that terrorists will detonate nuclear weapons once they acquire them is a prevalent one. The problem with this line of thinking is that it too easily strips away the strategic thought that al Qaeda puts into its violent behaviour. Al Qaeda has a strategy. [Middle East expert] Jerry Mark Long writes that its "long-term goals have been articulated in a multitude of venues and with remarkable consistency." It couches its war with the West as a "defensive" and "morally legitimate" one. It acts in accordance with a particular set of religious beliefs and is careful to behave in ways that remain within certain jurisprudential limitations. Al Qaeda is also sensitive to Muslim condemnation. The point is that there is some disagreement within al Qaeda with regards to the legitimacy and strategic utility of using nuclear weapons. One way the West might manipulate these debates is to take steps to heighten al Qaeda's concern that nuclear use will provoke a backlash among the wider Muslim audience. Doing that rests on spreading existing antinuclear norms and taboos among and within states.

In sum, Obama has done the world a service by calling for greater control over nuclear weapons and materials. Let's just make sure the discussion is built on fact rather than fiction.

CHAPTER 3

Are Ballistic Missile Defense Systems Necessary?

Chapter Preface

The delivery systems used to deliver nuclear bombs to distant targets are called ballistic missiles—projectiles that are guided in the first part of their flight but then fall freely as they approach their targets. For many decades, the United States has sought to develop an effective missile defense system to defend against missile-delivered nuclear attacks. America's missile defense program began shortly after World War II when the start of Cold War hostilities between the United States and the Soviet Union led both sides to actively pursue research on long-range missiles, as well as missile defense, as part of a growing nuclear arms race. Since then, the United States has spent billions trying to develop and perfect an effective missile defense system, including an effort in the 1980s proposed by the then president Ronald Reagan to produce a space-based missile defense program—a technologically complex and ultimately unsuccessful idea that was labeled Star Wars. In recent years, most military experts have abandoned their research support for spaced-based missile defense. Instead, they have turned their attention to whether US defensive missiles should be placed in Europe, the size of land- or sea-based systems, and the costs of missile defense.

Efforts to control the US-Soviet nuclear arms and missile race began after the election of US president Richard Nixon in 1968, when the two countries began discussions, called the Strategic Arms Limitation Talks (SALT). About two years later, these talks produced the Anti-Ballistic Missile (ABM) Treaty of 1972, which limited the United States and Soviet Union to two missile defense sites, each one limited to one hundred missile interceptors. The ABM Treaty was modified in 1974 to reduce the number of permissible sites to one for each country. The ABM Treaty limited the size of missile defense systems, but the United States continued to perfect its missile defense technology. By the early 1980s, the United States had developed a defensive missile that could destroy an attacking missile by physically colliding with it—a capability known as hit-to-kill.

Despite this achievement, US military analysts worried that improvements in the Soviet Union's offensive missiles could give them a first-strike capability that could significantly damage US strategic forces and still retain enough nuclear weapons to destroy America's cities. On March 23, 1983, President Ronald Reagan proposed the creation of the Strategic Defense Initiative (SDI), a program that was intended to defend the United States against attack from Soviet intercontinental ballistic missiles (ICBMs) by directing lasers at incoming missiles from both space- and earth-based stations. This idea was extremely ambitious because it would have required advanced technologies that had not yet been developed, and critics quickly dubbed the proposal Star Wars. Ultimately, the idea did turn out to be too difficult, and the system was canceled.

The SDI program has now been replaced by more realistic missile defense programs. One is called Terminal High Altitude Area Defense (THAAD), a US Army system designed to shoot down short, medium, and intermediate ballistic missiles using the hit-to-kill, physical impact approach first developed in the 1980s. THAAD is mobile and land based, allowing it to protect small areas either in the United States or in other countries, and it has been successful in six tests since 2006. However, THAAD would not be effective against long-range ICBMs and could not protect the entire United States from missile attack. Protecting all of the country from a limited missile attack was the job of another missile defense program called National Missile Defense (NMD). NMD used a land-based missile interceptor to destroy incoming ICBMs when they reentered the earth's atmosphere. Like THAAD, the NMD system would track incoming offensive missiles and then launch and guide intercepting missiles into them, but NMD had limited success, hitting its target only eight out of fifteen times in intercept tests. The system's name was changed to Ground-Based Midcourse Defense (GMD) in 2002. Neither THAAD nor GMD is designed to protect the United States against a large-scale nuclear attack from Russia or China, however. Instead, both systems are intended as a defense to smaller nuclear missile strikes from rogue countries like North Korea or Iran.

The idea of developing these missile defense systems has been politically controversial. In order to develop NMD/GMD, which would have violated the 1972 ABM Treaty, President George W. Bush announced in 2001 that the United States planned to withdraw from the treaty. This marked the first time in history that the United States had withdrawn from a major international arms treaty, and critics feared it would jeopardize other arms agreements as well as US relations with Russia and China. US officials reassured Russian and Chinese officials, however, that the missile defense was not directed toward them, but rather was needed to protect the United States from rogue nations. The Bush administration proposed that the GMD system should have fifty-four missile interceptors— forty-four in Alaska and California and ten in Poland.

President Barack Obama's administration has continued to fund missile defense and has increased funding for a ship-based missile defense program called Aegis. However, the president has been criticized for reducing the size of the GMD system to thirty interceptors and deciding to cancel the plan to position GMD interceptors in Poland. The viewpoints in this chapter provide differing views about the need for missile defense.

The Greatest Strategic Threat to the United States Is an Attack by a Nuclear-Armed Missile

Missilethreat.com

Missilethreat.com, a project of the Claremont Institute, is a website that outlines the strategic defense of the United States in relation to the proliferation of ballistic missiles.

The greatest strategic threat to the United States is an attack by one or more ballistic missiles armed with nuclear or other weapons of mass destruction. Today, the United States remains completely vulnerable to this form of attack.

Missilethreat.com is dedicated to explaining this threat and the urgent need for robust and layered missile defenses. Systems based on land, sea, air, and in space, which are capable of intercepting a missile during any phase of its flight, are necessary to provide for the common defense. . . .

The Threat from China

In 2005, the Pentagon [U.S. defense headquarters] expressed its concerns over the speed of China's military buildup. While official Chinese sources claim that defense spending constitutes approximately $30 billion, the Pentagon estimates that China's defense sector could receive up to $90 billion in 2005, which makes China the third largest defense spender in the world after the United States and Russia, and the largest in Asia. Over the past decade, China has deployed these resources to build a technically sophisticated ballistic missile force: short-range missiles to prevent Taiwan's independence; medium-range missiles to gain regional supremacy in East Asia; and long-range missiles to deter the United States from interfering in the first two objectives. China sees the United States as a strategic target and includes ICBM [intercontinental ballistic missile] testing in military exercises aimed at Taiwan. In addition, China continues to export its missile technology to Pakistan, Iran, North Korea, and others. . . .

China is, along with Russia, one of the main proliferators of nuclear and missile technology. The United States has previously sanctioned several Chinese companies for transferring missile technology to Pakistan, Iran, North Korea, and others. Despite official denials from both parties, there is overwhelming evidence that China has exported at least 30 M-11s to Pakistan in contravention of the Missile Technology Control Regime. China also appears to have reached an agreement with Iran to supply components and/or production technology to produce the M-11. Some reports suggest that this production technology includes both propellant and guidance system facilities. China is also known to have built a production facility near Semnan in Iran which has been producing Oghab artillery rockets and the Iran-130 BSRBM since 1987.

Russia's nuclear and ballistic missile arsenal remains the single greatest strategic threat to the United States.

According to recent reports, China is aiding Syrian missile programs to extend the range of Scud missiles from short to medium and intermediate. In July 2004, U.S. Secretary of Energy Spencer Abraham announced that Libya possessed blueprints and all components for a Chinese nuclear warhead. China is also known to have sold some . . . CSS-2s with conventional warheads to Saudi Arabia, which are maintained and operated by Chinese personnel. A further Chinese program, the CSS-8 (M-7) SRBM is a modified Russian SA-2 surface-to-air missile with solid-fuelled motors. China embarked on this program after stealing Soviet SA-2s destined for North Vietnam via the Chinese rail network in 1966 or 1967 and reverse engineering them as the HQ-2 SAM. China exported at least 20 CSS-8s to Iran in 1992, although their relatively short range means that they would be useful only in defense of Iranian territory or for limited strikes against neighboring countries. . . .

The Threat from India

India's security environment is dominated by its mistrust of Pakistan, with whom it has fought three wars in the past 40 years, as well as its competition for regional influence with China, with whom it fought a border war in 1962. A combination of high defense spending and considerable technical expertise has made India's military-industrial base one of the most diversified in the developing world.

India began its Integrated Guided Missile Development Program (IGMDP) in 1983 with the aim of achieving self-sufficiency in missile development and production. The IGMDP's offensive component includes Prithvi short-range and Agni intermediate-range ballistic missiles. There is also speculation about the existence of an intercontinental ballistic missile program known as the Surya. In addition, India is currently developing Dhanush sea-launched ballistic missiles and BrahMos cruise missiles. . . .

The Threat from Russia

The collapse and reconstitution of the Soviet Union did not lead to its disarmament. Russia still possesses a powerful nuclear arsenal—thousands of land-based intercontinental ballistic missiles (ICBMs), sea-launched ballistic missiles (SLBMs), and sea-launched cruise missiles (SLCMs), armed and targeted at the United States. Moreover, Russia continues to modernize and expand this arsenal despite its economic problems and perceived military weakness. In recent years, reports have indicated that security at Russia's nuclear/missile facilities is breaking down, thus elevating the chances that a warhead or missile will fall into the hands of terrorists or rogue military elements. Finally, Russia is among the world's most rampant proliferators of missile technology. For these reasons, Russia's nuclear and ballistic missile arsenal remains the single greatest strategic threat to the United States. . . .

In addition to the threat of a conventional Russian nuclear attack, the United States is also threatened by negligent security at Russia's nuclear/missile facilities, as well as rampant proliferation of ballistic missile technology and expertise to rogue nations and terrorist-sponsoring states.

The security of the Russian nuclear arsenal constitutes a serious threat to the United States. Should a missile or warhead get into the hands of rogue elements of the Russian military, a launch is possible. Former secretary of defense Robert McNamara has warned as recently as April 2004 that a nuclear attack from Russia is a very real scenario today, whether by accident or intention. Even a benign Russia that miscalculates can destroy America in less than half an hour. Moreover, there remains the possibility that a loose Russian WMD [weapon of mass destruction] might fall into the hands of Islamist terrorists, such as those operating in Chechnya and the former Soviet republics in central Asia. In May 2004, Nikolai Patrushev, head of the Russian Federal Security Service (FSB), stated his concern that these terrorist organizations could gain possession of loose Russian nuclear weapons, as well as other WMDs.

Besides the direct threat of Russian ballistic technology falling into the hands of terrorists, the more indirect threat of Russia's proliferation of nuclear and missile technology to rogue states remains a cause of significant concern. Along with China, Russia is the greatest source of ballistic missile proliferation, evidence of which is well documented yet underappreciated. Reports that Russia is helping Iran develop a nuclear bomb, or that Russian scientists assisted North Korea in developing mobile intermediate range missiles should come as no surprise, but rather as a continuation of the use of proxies which so characterized the Soviet era.

Most worrisome is Russia's strategic relationship with Iran, which appears to have grown in recent years. Through this relationship, Russia is able to project its power into the Middle East, which it fears that the U.S. will dominate through its efforts in Iraq and Afghanistan. Most notably, the Iranian Shahab-3 and Shahab-4 medium-range ballistic missiles were built with Russian technology and expertise. In March 2004, Stephen Rademaker, U.S. assistant secretary of state for arms control, stated that Russia continues to contribute to the proliferation of medium- and short-range ballistic missile systems and technology to Iran. That September, the U.S. sanctioned three Russian, Belarusian, and Ukrainian companies for exporting technology and materials to Iran.

Beyond Iran, Russia has also been involved with two other Middle Eastern nations: Iraq and Syria. In March 2004, the *New York Times* described in detail how Russian ballistic missile technology aided Saddam Hussein's Iraqi missile programs until not too long before the 2003 Iraq war. In direct violation of United Nations sanctions, Russian engineers reportedly worked on the Iraqi program both in Moscow and in Baghdad. In January 2005, the Russian newspaper *Kommersant* reported that Russia allegedly intended to sell a number of missile systems to Syria, including the export version of the SS-26 Iskander missile, which has a reported range of 280 km [kilometers] and would be able to strike nearly all of Israel, as well as U.S. military regional assets.

Russia has also been involved in North Korea's missile development program. In August 2004, Jane's *Defence Weekly* reported that North Korea was deploying two forms of a new missile system, capable of striking U.S. military forces in Guam and Japan and also the continental United States. The new missile is believed to be based primarily upon the Russian SS-N-6 submarine launched ballistic missile, as well as some SS-N-5 technology and assistance from the Russian missile manufacturer VP Makeyev Design Bureau. The land-based mobile version of the missile has an estimated range of missile 2,500–4,000 km, and the submarine- or ship-based version some 2,500 km or more. . . .

The Threat from Syria

For the past half century, Syria's overriding military objective has been the destruction of Israel. Yet on the battlefield, Syria has been defeated by the Israeli Defense Forces in every conventional military engagement, most spectacularly in 1967, 1973, and 1982. A realistic assessment of its conventional military performance has led Syria to adopt a new four-track strategy in hopes of thwarting Israel by other means: (a) state sponsorship of terrorism, (b) a quest for weapons of mass destruction, (c) a steady buildup of offensive and defense missile systems, and (d) active weapons proliferation. For these reasons, although Syria's conventional forces remain inadequate, the unconventional threat from Syria has become considerable.

Since the early 1980s, Damascus has openly provided material and political backing to the militant Islamic terrorist group Hezbollah, gaining Syria a prominent place on the U.S. list of state sponsors of terrorism. In its ceaseless struggle against Israel, Hezbollah has committed terrorist acts against Israelis and Americans, including the suicide bombings of the U.S. embassy and the U.S. Marine barracks in Beirut, as well as the firing of low-flying Katyusha rockets at Israeli civilian populations. In addition to its support for Hezbollah, Syria aids and abets radical Palestinian terrorist groups such as Hamas and Islamic Jihad, which have been largely responsible for the escalation of the Israeli-Palestinian conflict in recent years.

In addition, Syria has actively sought to acquire weapons of mass destruction. According to a 2003 CIA [Central Intelligence Agency] report, Damascus already has a stockpile of the nerve agent Sarin, but apparently is trying to develop more toxic and persistent nerve agents as well as biological weapons with the aid of foreign sources. John Bolton, [former] undersecretary of state for arms control, recently testified before the House international relations committee and reiterated that Syria has acquired "what is now one of the most advanced Arab chemical weapons capabilities" and is "continuing to develop an offensive biological weapons capability." In addition to this chemical and biological weaponry, the CIA notes that Syria has a nuclear research center at Dayr al-Hajar and has access to considerable Russian expertise, should it consider pursuing nuclear weapons.

Syria's sponsorship of terrorism and quest for weapons of mass destruction is especially troubling due to its steady buildup of offensive ballistic missile systems. Syria's missile program, which dates back to the 1970s, includes Scud B, C, and D variants, SS-21s, M-9 and M-11 variants, and Frog-7s. It is currently one of the largest arsenals of offensive weapons in the Middle East, thanks largely to Russia, China, and North Korea. Assistance from the former Soviet Union has included sales of Scuds, SS-21s, and Frog-7s. In recent years, China has sent diplomatic and technological delegations to Syria to discuss strategies for boosting Syria's missile capabilities, the focus of which has been to extend the range of Syria's Scuds from short to medium and even intermediate. North Korea has concentrated on helping Syria to establish a solid-propellant rocket motor development and production capability.

In recent months, reports have indicated that Russia plans to sell a number of new missile systems to Syria, including the made-for-export SS-26 Iskander missile, the S-300 PMU-2 air and missile defense system, and the shoulder-fired SA-18 Igla anti-aircraft missile. Most worrisome is the SS-26 Iskander's reported range of 280 kilometers, which would allow Syria to attack nearly all of Israel. Syria is also negotiating the purchase of the Russian S-400 air and missile defense system, said to be comparable or superior to the U.S. Patriot PAC-3 interceptor. Including these recent developments, it is apparent that Syria's offensive arsenal, if armed with chemical or biological weapons and protected by a sizeable air and missile defense shield, poses a serious threat to Israel, as well as U.S. forces stationed in the Middle East, and even a democratic Iraq.

In addition to its own missile capabilities, Syria engages in dangerous proliferation behavior. In January 2004 and afterward, Syria sent Scud C and D missiles as well as chemical weapons to the Sudan. The arms shipments were recently revealed when Sudanese president Omar al-Bashir, fearing U.S. sanctions, ordered the missiles and chemical weapons removed from his country. In addition, it has been revealed by Major General [Aharon] Ze'evi Farkash, head of the Israeli Defense Forces intelligence branch, that Hezbollah recently sought to acquire short-range ballistic missiles armed with chemical weapons from Syria. Farkash noted that Hezbollah might already have as many as 30 missiles that are capable of traveling 215 kilometers.

Taken together, the threat from Syria looms large. Until Damascus abandons its state sponsorship of terrorism, WMD programs, steady buildup of offensive and defensive missile systems, and active weapons proliferation, it will remain a significant cause for concern.

The United States Must Have a Viable Missile Defense System

Mackenzie Eaglen

Mackenzie Eaglen is a research fellow for national security studies at the Allison Center for Foreign Policy Studies, a public policy project of the Heritage Foundation, a conservative think tank.

Some arguments are worth repeating. Take missile defense. The basic justification for developing this weapon system has not changed much since President Reagan proposed it in 1983. But the threats have changed. In fact, the threats we face are more varied and are evolving at a faster rate than at any other time in our history. Ten years ago, for example, few people knew what an improvised explosive device was. Today, they are the weapon of choice for insurgents in Afghanistan, Iraq and elsewhere around the world. Recent conflicts have also demonstrated the devastating effects of cyber and denial-of-service attacks; and more unsettled state actors are partnering with subgroups to cause trouble. As the predictability of the kinds of threats we face has diminished, military planners have been forced to prepare to defend against virtually everything. Since no one would secure a home by locking all the windows but leaving the front door open, the U.S. shouldn't choose to remain vulnerable to a ballistic missile attack—particularly since these weapons can be armed with a chemical, biological or nuclear weapon.

It only takes 30 minutes for a ballistic missile to reach U.S. shores from anywhere in the world. We would barely have time to lament our lack of missile defenses before an attacking weapon was upon us. Since the enemy always "gets a vote," U.S. leaders need only pay attention to what others are saying and doing to validate the need for a comprehensive missile defense system to protect Americans.

The Threats We Face

Iran will likely achieve nuclear status in the near future, and the world has limited visibility into their program and even less into their leaders' intentions. The International Atomic Energy Agency [IAEA] is having difficulty developing a comprehensive picture of Iran's nuclear program, but officials believe Iran may be working on affixing a nuclear warhead to one of its growing classes of ballistic missiles. Even the U.S. military estimates that Iran will be capable of fielding an intercontinental ballistic missile by 2015. Numbers tell the rest of the story. In just the past decade, the number of nuclear states around the globe has grown from six to nine. Meanwhile a total of 28 countries have ballistic missile capabilities. Some are rapidly improving their arsenals with help from other states. China, for example, has shown it is capable of targeting U.S. satellites with ballistic missiles and electromagnetic pulse warheads. In January 2007, China launched an intercontinental ballistic missile (ICBM) at one of its own satellites. The Chinese referred to the test as an experiment and not a deliberate anti-satellite test. Nevertheless, the action proved Chinese capabilities and demonstrates their potential for growth.

North Korea has some 1,000 missiles and is selling them to other countries. It has tested at least 25 missiles with ranges of up to 1,200 miles. This means North Korean missiles are capable of reaching South Korea and Japan. Its leaders are also developing a new ICBM with a minimum range of 3,700 miles that could hit Alaska and some parts of Hawaii if it functioned at its full capacity. Judging by capabilities (missile arsenals) as well as intentions (official statements from world leaders), the need for a U.S. missile defense system is clear. Of course, missile defense offers more than protection of Americans at home and abroad. The purely defensive system also provides security assurance and comfort to friends and allies. Our investment in missile defense is what prevents others from building up their own arsenals and reduces their perceived need to acquire additional weapons. The United States today provides security for more than 30 countries around the world and thus prevents these nations from pursuing large missile programs of their own. As a result, the number of weapons throughout the world has decreased, which is a desirable outcome. The bottom line is that missile defense decreases the importance and utility of ballistic missiles. This dramatically limits their attractiveness to potential enemies, given that such an attack would more than likely fail.

What's Needed Here at Home

A comprehensive, multilayered missile defense should be a priority. And the vast majority of Americans support the program. A poll conducted by Opinion Research Corporation this past May [2010] reveals that 88 percent of the respondents believe that the federal government should field a system for countering ballistic missiles capable of carrying weapons of mass destruction. However, many also mistakenly believe we already have what is needed to defeat a range of threats.

President Obama's "phased adaptive approach" for missile defense has some merits but also has unnecessarily slowed the program while the threat has remained the same. Iran may be capable of launching a long-range missile by 2015, yet the U.S. missile defense program will not be capable of defeating this type of threat until 2020. The Department of Defense has requested $9.9 billion in the fiscal year 2011 budget for the missile defense program, with $8.4 billion of that going to the Missile Defense Agency (MDA). One notable improvement is the $2.2 billion request for the sea-based Aegis ballistic missile defense system—an 11 percent increase over the previous year. While the MDA budget shows an increase over the previous year's request, it still falls nearly $1 billion short of President [George W.] Bush's final request in fiscal year 2009. The administration's plan for missile defense has four stages that continue through 2020. The program includes both land- and sea-based interceptors. Ultimately, the fourth phase would move the system beyond regional defense and protect the entire U.S. homeland against an ICBM attack. Unfortunately, the administration has cut back on other integral parts of the comprehensive program. The number of ground-based interceptors in Alaska and California has been cut from 44 to 30, the planned "third site" for missile defense in Poland and the Czech Republic was cancelled, and funding has been eliminated for space-based interceptors. For a truly effective and comprehensive system, the land, sea and air components must be strengthened. First, the administration should reinstate the original plan to field 44 ground-based midcourse defense interceptors in Alaska and California. As the number of countries that possess ballistic missiles grows alongside the size of many arsenals, additional interceptors are necessary. Congress should add $200 million to the missile defense budget to begin restoring the planned interceptors here in the U.S.

Additional funding is also needed for the successful sea-based system. Congress should bolster the Aegis ballistic missile defense in 2011 to accelerate and expand both the development and procurement of the Aegis weapons system and the Standard Missile 3 (SM-3) family of interceptors. One example involves funding smaller and lighter vehicles for the SM-3 interceptors. An optimal speed for the interceptor is six to seven kilometers per hour, which can best be achieved by using these lighter vehicles. This would ensure that the interceptors can protect larger areas and allow them to intercept missiles in the first stage of launch all while engaging missiles with the longest ranges. The complete lack of investment in space-based interceptors and minimal funding for space activities needs to be reversed. There are substantial benefits to a robust space-based system. The Airborne Laser program (which has already been proven successful at striking a missile in the first, or "boost," phase) should be resurrected. This is important because during the boost phase, the missile is still over the enemy's land. If intercepted at this point, it significantly reduces the risk of any spillover effects.

Indeed, as Lt. General (Ret.) Trey Obering has said, missile defense is similar to an insurance policy for the protection of all Americans—except, of course, it's a much better investment. If, say, you get into a car accident, only then does your insurance help you.

But with missile defense, having a system in place could prevent an enemy attack from ever reaching Washington, New York, Dallas, Miami, Seattle or Los Angeles. It's peace of mind worth investing in.

It's also proof that old arguments are often worth repeating, particularly when—as in the case of missile defense—they are correct.

A Full-Coverage Missile Defense System Is Needed to Protect the United States

R. James Woolsey and Rebeccah Heinrichs

R. James Woolsey is a former director of Central Intelligence and a board member at the Foundation for Defense of Democracies where Rebeccah Heinrichs, a former manager of the House Bi-Partisan Missile Defense Caucus, is an adjunct fellow.

In a June 27 [2010] interview on ABC's *This Week*, CIA [Central Intelligence Agency] director Leon Panetta warned that it could be a mere two years before Iran is able to threaten other states with nuclear warheads mounted on ballistic missiles. When discussing the new U.S. sanctions against Iran recently signed into law by President Barack Obama, Mr. Panetta said, "Will it deter them from their ambitions with regards to nuclear capability? Probably not."

The Threat from Iran

Three months ago the Defense Intelligence Agency reported that by 2015 Iran, with help from North Korea or Russia, could field an intercontinental ballistic missile (ICBM) capable of reaching the East Coast of the United States. This is by no means far-fetched. In early 2009, the Iranians successfully launched their first homegrown satellite into orbit. In March of that same year, Gen. Michael Maples, then director of the Defense Intelligence Agency, told a Senate panel that Iran's successful satellite launch "shows progress in mastering the technology needed to produce ICBMs [intercontinental

R. James Woolsey and Rebeccah Heinrichs, "Iran and the Missile Defense Imperative," online.wsj.com, July 14, 2010. Reprinted from the Wall Street Journal © 2010 Dow Jones & Company. All rights reserved. Copyright © 2010 by James Woolsey and Rebeccah Heinrichs. Reproduced by permission.

ballistic missiles]." Earlier this year Iran successfully orbited a second satellite with an ICBM-class ballistic missile.

Gen. Maples is right. If you can launch a satellite into orbit you are very close to being able to hit a target halfway around the world. That's why the Soviet launch of Sputnik so shocked the U.S. intelligence community in 1957. When a country is the most active state sponsor of terrorism, and its leaders routinely endorse slogans like "Death to Israel" and "Death to America," we should take it seriously when they pursue the capabilities to make their dreams a reality.

A December 2009 missile launch proved Iran has already obtained the ability to reach Israel. Given [Iranian] President Mahmoud Ahmadinejad's and other Iranian leaders' millenarian fanaticism, it would be most imprudent to rely on nuclear deterrence alone to protect us. If Tehran were to achieve a nuclear missile capability, it could hold American cities hostage—unless, that is, the U.S. builds a robust and comprehensive ballistic missile defense.

U.S. Missile Defenses

Our current missile shield will have 26 ground-based interceptors based in Alaska, in addition to the four based in California, by the end of this year. These are part of an initial defense architecture designed to protect against missiles launched from North Korea. These interceptors could provide some protection from missiles launched from Iran toward our East Coast, but the margin for error would be unacceptably small.

Moreover, once Tehran can build one or two functioning ICBMs, it can build many more. As Defense Secretary Robert Gates testified before a Senate panel on June 17, "If Iran were actually to launch a missile attack on Europe, it wouldn't be just one or two missiles, or a handful." We need a defensive system that has full coverage, especially of the U.S. homeland, and that can add interceptors easily to cope with an Iranian ICBM buildup.

That's why the [George W.] Bush administration proposed building a missile-defense site in Europe in addition to those already in place in Alaska and California. This would provide cities on the East Coast, our troops abroad, and our allies in Europe added protection from an Iranian missile attack.

But last September [2009] the Obama administration scrapped the Bush plan and replaced it with one called the Phased Adaptive Approach, which is less capable of dealing with threats against U.S. territory. This plan entails deploying mobile systems to Europe to intercept short-range missiles. The Defense Department would gradually upgrade these systems, but the plan offers no added protection for the U.S. until 2020. That's almost certainly too little too late.

Our vulnerabilities don't stop there. If Iran were to launch a nuclear-armed missile from a ship near one of our coasts— say a primitive Scud from a fishing boat—we would have very little warning and no protection. Defending the homeland against this threat would require a substantial deployment in and near the U.S. of the type of mobile systems that the administration plans to deploy in Europe.

Further, if the Iranians were to detonate even a primitive nuclear warhead over the United States, it could send out an electromagnetic pulse (EMP) destroying the electric grid and electrical systems across a wide swath of U.S. territory. Iranian military writings show the mullahs recognize the potential of this kind of attack. Depending on where it occurred and how large the warhead was, an EMP attack could cause large-scale fatalities and unimaginable economic devastation. Defending against this kind of threat requires defensive systems that can intercept an attacking ballistic missile while it is still ascending. But the Obama administration has no specific plans to develop and deploy ascent-phase interceptors in Europe.

A Need to Reevaluate Strategy

Given the growing Iranian threat, the Obama administration should reevaluate its missile-defense strategy. The U.S. should deploy as many interceptors as possible in Alaska and should plan for an emergency deployment of a third site either in Europe or on the East Coast. Moreover, as Iran continues to improve its missiles, and the White House negotiates agreements to host radars and other missile-defense assets in Europe, the administration should make contingency plans for rapid deployment of mobile defenses, including ascent-phase interceptors, to protect us here at home.

Above all the Obama administration should clarify to the U.S. Senate and the Russian government that neither the new U.S.-Russian Strategic Arms Reduction Treaty nor commitments made during the negotiation process will in any way limit our ability to protect ourselves against an Iranian nuclear attack.

The United States Needs a Space-Based Missile Defense System

Institute for Foreign Policy Analysis

The Institute for Foreign Policy Analysis is an independent research organization specializing in national security, foreign policy, and defense planning issues.

Missile defense has entered a new era. The decades-long debate over whether to protect the American people from the threat of ballistic missile attack has been settled— and settled unequivocally in favor of missile defense. The rigid constraints of the Anti-Ballistic Missile (ABM) Treaty, which made the construction of effective antimissile capabilities impossible during the decades of the Cold War, are now a thing of the past. What remains an open question is what shape the American missile defense system will take in the years ahead.

Threats to the United States from Ballistic Missiles

Yet there is ample reason for concern. The threat environment confronting the United States in the twenty-first century differs fundamentally from that of the Cold War. An unprecedented number of international actors have now acquired—or are seeking to acquire—ballistic missiles and weapons of mass destruction. Rogue states, chief among them North Korea and Iran, have placed a premium on the acquisition of nuclear, chemical and biological weapons and the means to deliver them, and are moving rapidly toward that goal. Russia and China, traditional competitors of the United

States, continue to expand the range and sophistication of their strategic arsenals. And a number of asymmetric threats—including the possibility of weapons of mass destruction (WMD) acquisition by terrorist groups or the decimation of American critical infrastructure as a result of electromagnetic pulse (EMP)—now pose a direct threat to the safety and security of the United States. Moreover, the number and sophistication of these threats are evolving at a pace that no longer allows the luxury of long lead times for the development and deployment of defenses.

The Need for Space-Based Missile Defense

In order to address these increasingly complex and multifaceted dangers, the United States must deploy a system that is capable of comprehensive protection of the American homeland as well as its overseas forces and its allies from the threat of ballistic missile attack. Over the long term, U.S. defenses also must be able to dissuade would-be missile possessors from costly investments in missile technologies, and to deter future adversaries from confronting the United States with WMD or ballistic missiles. Our strategic objective should be to make it impossible for any adversary to influence U.S. decision making in times of conflict through the use of ballistic missiles or WMD blackmail.

These priorities necessitate the deployment of a system capable of constant defense against a wide range of threats in all phases of flight: boost, midcourse, and terminal. A layered system—encompassing ground-based (area and theater antimissile assets) and sea-based capabilities—would provide multiple opportunities to destroy incoming missiles in various phases of flight. A truly global capability, however, cannot be achieved without a missile defense architecture incorporating interdiction capabilities in space as one of its key operational elements. In the twenty-first century, space has replaced the seas as the ultimate frontier for commerce, technology and national security.

The benefits of space-based defense are manifold. The deployment of a robust global missile defense that includes space-based interdiction capabilities will make more expensive, and therefore less attractive, the foreign development of technologies needed to overcome it, particularly with regard to ballistic missiles. Indeed, the enduring lesson of the ABM Treaty era is that the *absence* of defenses, rather than their presence, empowers the development of offensive technologies that can threaten American security and the lives of American citizens. And access to space, as well as space control, is key to future U.S. efforts to provide disincentives to an array of actors seeking such power.

Current vs. Missile Defenses

So far, however, the United States has stopped short of putting these principles into practice. Rather, the missile defense system that has emerged since President [George W.] Bush's historic December 2002 announcement of an "initial set" of missile defense capabilities provides extremely limited coverage, and no global capability. Instead, by the administration's own admission, it is intended as a limited defense against a small, rogue state threat scenario. Left unaddressed are the evolving missile arsenals of—and potential missile threats from—strategic competitors such as Russia and China as well as terrorists launching short-range missiles such as Scuds from offshore vessels.

The key impediments to the development of a more robust layered system that includes space-based interdiction assets have been more political than technological. A small but vocal minority has so far succeeded in driving the debate against both space-based defense and missile defense writ large. The outcome has been that political considerations have by and large dictated technical behavior, with the goal of developing the most technologically sound and cost-effective defenses subordinated to other interests.

A symptom of this problem is the fact that, for all of its commitment to protecting the United States from ballistic missile attack, the administration has so far done little to revive the cutting-edge technologies developed under the administrations of Presidents Ronald Reagan and George H. W. Bush—technologies that produced the most effective, least costly ways to defend the U.S. homeland, its deployed troops and its international partners from the threat of ballistic missile attack. The most impressive of these initiatives was undoubtedly Brilliant Pebbles. By 1992, that system—entailing the deployment of a constellation of small, advanced kill vehicles in space—had developed a cheap, effective means of destroying enemy ballistic missiles in all modes of flight. Yet in the early 1990s, along with a number of other promising programs, it fell victim to a systematic eradication of space-based technologies that marked the closing years of the twentieth century and still plagues the opening years of the twenty-first century.

Security Implications

The current state of affairs surrounding missile defense carries profound implications for the safety and security of the United States, and its role on the world stage in the decades to come. Without the means to dissuade, deter and defeat the growing number of strategic adversaries now arrayed against it, the United States will be unable to maintain its status of global leadership. The creation of effective defenses against ballistic missile attack remains central to this task.

Historically, it is evident that the major geopolitical options that become available have been exploited by one nation or another. Those nations that are most successful in recognizing and acting on such options have become dominant. Others who have failed or have consciously decided not to do so are relegated to inferior political status. A salient case in point is ocean navigation and exploration. The Chinese were the first to become preeminent in this retrospectively pivotal area during the early Ming dynasty. However, domestic politics—strongly reminiscent of missile defense politics in the United States of the past several decades—induced this great national head to be dissipated, with historic consequences felt until the present day, a full half millennium later. The subsequent assumption by Portugal of this leading maritime role resulted in geopolitical preeminence that was eventually lost to other European powers.

In the twenty-first century, maintenance of its present lead in space may indeed be pivotal to the basic geopolitical, military, and economic status of the United States. Consolidation of the preeminent U.S. position in space akin to Britain's dominance of the oceans in the nineteenth century is not an option, but rather a necessity, for if not the United States, some other nation, or nations, will aspire to this role, as several others already do. For the United States space is a crucially important twenty-first-century geopolitical setting that includes a global missile defense.

Missile Defense Systems Are Expensive and Do Not Work

Tom Sauer

Tom Sauer is assistant professor in international politics at the Universiteit Antwerpen (Belgium), and he is author of the book Nuclear Inertia: US Weapons Policy After the Cold War *(2005).*

What to do with a defense instrument that does not work in practice, agitates neighboring regional powers, and costs a lot of money in times of economic crisis? Common sense would suggest you abandon it. NATO [North Atlantic Treaty Organization] however, has a different idea. As part of the NATO Strategic Concept review to be finalized at the end of November [2009] at the Lisbon [Portugal] summit, NATO Secretary-General Anders Fogh Rasmussen has proposed to adopt missile defense as a mission.

Initially, NATO's Star Wars was linked to the withdrawal of U.S. tactical nuclear weapons in Europe. Since European allies perceive the nuclear umbrella as a symbol of transatlantic solidarity, opponents of the withdrawal required an alternative burden-sharing instrument: missile defense. Replacing offensive by defensive weapons system might even be easier to sell to a skeptical European public.

Even though the withdrawal of U.S. nukes has not yet taken place, missile defense is likely to move forward anyway.

The Obama Plan

If missile defense is accepted as a "new mission" in Lisbon, President [Barack] Obama's missile defense plans that were made public in September 2009 will be merged with NATO's Active Layered Theatre Ballistic Missile Defence system. The latter, designed to protect NATO troops in the field against short-range ballistic missiles, is supposed to be finished at the end of this year. If the new mission is accepted, NATO's objective significantly expands beyond protecting troops in the field to protecting all of NATO's territory. For this expansion to take place, NATO's system will be plugged into the U.S. facilities in Europe initially established to protect the United States alone. Obama rejected [George W.] Bush's plan to install 10 interceptors in Poland and a radar in the Czech Republic. However, Obama's replacement plan does not significantly differ in magnitude from the Bush vision. The Obama administration plans to put into place SM-3 interceptors on Aegis ships in the Mediterranean, two of which have already arrived. In the next stage, the administration plans next year to build an X-band radar station either in Bulgaria or in Turkey and a warning center in the Czech Republic. In 2015, the United States would then station interceptors on land, probably in Romania. These defensive interceptors are supposed to defend against short- and medium-range ballistic missiles.

The missile shield doesn't work. Every country with offensive ballistic missiles can easily produce countermeasures like decoys or false warheads.

Beginning in 2018, the United States would place more powerful interceptors against intermediate-range ballistic missiles in Poland. The plan would be finalized in 2020 with defensive missiles capable of intercepting intercontinental missiles.

Why the Plan Doesn't Work

There are, however, two objections to a NATO missile shield. The technology is not ready, and Russia is angry about missile defense on its borders.

The missile shield doesn't work. Every country with offensive ballistic missiles can easily produce countermeasures like decoys or false warheads, which makes it nearly impossible for defensive interceptors to strike targets outside the atmosphere (exo-atmospheric). Both the SM-3 missiles on Aegis ships and on European territory face this problem.

The proposed NATO missile shield does not improve geo-strategic stability.

The U.S. Missile Defense Agency claims that the tests with the Aegis SM-3 missiles have been successful. Everything depends of course on how "success" is defined. The Patriot missiles—which are endo-atmospheric and therefore less sophisticated—were touted as successfully destroying Saddam Hussein's Scuds in 1991. But only three out of more than 50 Patriots effectively destroyed their targets. Formally, the Pentagon had defined "success" as "a Patriot and a Scud that passed in the sky." Similar misleading practices disguise the real performances of the SM-3 missiles, the backbone of the missile shield in Europe. According to recent scientific analysis by George Lewis (Cornell University) and Ted Postol (MIT [Massachusetts Institute of Technology]), published in the magazine *Arms Control Today*, nine out of 10 "successful" intercepts with SM-3 missiles were not successful. Sometimes the interceptors hit the offensive missile, but failed to destroy the warhead. Often these warheads then continued on their way in the direction of the target.

Even if this system encounters such technical problems, Russian strategists have to assume that they work. When Obama talks about a phased approach, which would extend the system in the future, Russian fears only mount. The Russian nuclear arsenal is both quantitatively and qualitatively small compared to U.S. capabilities. According to one estimate, if the Russian arsenal is not on alert, Russia will only have six surviving nuclear weapons after an American first strike. If U.S. nuclear primacy is bolstered by a missile defense shield, it would not be surprising that some Russian planners are panicking.

In short, the proposed NATO missile shield does not improve geostrategic stability. Further bilateral nuclear arms reductions with Russia may be hampered as well. This reasoning applies even more to China, which has a nuclear arsenal less than one-tenth of Russia's.

American taxpayers have spent $150 billion for a system that has yet to work in real time. NATO Secretary-General Rasmussen now wants European NATO member states to contribute to this system for the first time. Are we Europeans expected to bail out NATO's $600 million budget deficit and sponsor Star Wars as well?

Missile Defense Offers a False Promise of Protection from Nuclear Attack

Pavel Podvig

Pavel Podvig is a physicist trained at the Moscow Institute of Physics and Technology who works as a research associate at Stanford University's Center for International Security and Cooperation.

Editor's note: On September 17, 2009, President Barack Obama announced that the United States would not be placing missile defense installations in the Czech Republic or Poland.

Of the many security quagmires confronting President Barack Obama, perhaps the most challenging is how he navigates the [George W.] Bush administration's decision to place missile defense installations in Eastern Europe. As a candidate, Obama didn't rule out keeping the Bush plan to put a missile defense radar in the Czech Republic and interceptors in Poland, but he did place the onus on the technology—i.e., it had to be viable. True to his campaign promise, upon taking office, he ordered a review of the program, which is about to be completed.

No matter how critical the report is—and most expect it to be highly skeptical of the Bush plan—it won't be easy for Obama to reverse course on European missile defense. Poland and the Czech Republic would hate to see their 15 minutes of fame end as key U.S. allies when it comes to missile defense, and other NATO [North Atlantic Treaty Organization] allies would certainly wonder how seriously the United States takes its commitments. And if the change goes too far in accommodating Russian concerns, Republicans would be all too happy to accuse Obama of appeasement. As a result, Obama may make only minor modifications to the Bush plan—the radar, for example, might stay in the Czech Republic, but the interceptors could be moved offshore or to a less controversial location such as somewhere in the Balkans.

Problems with Missile Defense

More largely, it will be tough for Obama to let go of missile defense because until now, the discussion has been framed in such a way that it's implicitly assumed that missile defense is a fundamentally useful thing—as long as it can be made efficient and built at reasonable cost without damaging the prospect for nuclear disarmament, of course. In short, the argument often is that the current missile defense system is flawed, but if those flaws could be solved, missile defense would be a great boon to international security. Missile defense proponents, of course, go much further, stating that missile defense provides a reliable (and some insist the only) way to counter emerging missile threats. The notion of missile defense as a good thing even entered the nuclear abolition debate earlier this year, with many experts ready to grant it a useful role at the final stages of disarmament, arguing that it might provide protection against those who cheat the system and attempt to build/use a nuclear weapon.

In a real confrontation, missile defense would be irrelevant at best.

The fundamental problem with this argument is that missile defense will never live up to these expectations. Let me say that again: Missile defense will never make a shred of difference when it comes to its primary mission—protecting a country from the threat of a nuclear missile attack. That isn't to say that advanced sensors and interceptors someday won't be able to deal with sophisticated missiles and decoys. They probably will. But again, this won't overcome the fundamental challenge of keeping a nation safe against a nuclear threat, because it would take only a small probability of success to make such a threat credible while missile defense would need to offer absolute certainty of protection to truly be effective.

Missile Defense After the Cold War

This was fairly easy to grasp during the Cold War. At that time, it was clear that no defense could realistically protect people against thousands of warheads. But now that the Cold War is over and the threat involves a handful of warheads (if that many), the goal of building a working missile defense system seems within reach. Indeed, how hard would it be to intercept a rudimentary missile launched by North Korea? The answer seems simple: Not easy, but definitely doable. But it's the wrong question to ask. Instead, we should ask: Would missile defense change Washington's strategic calculation in a potential conflict with North Korea or Iran? The answer to this question is a firm no.

In a real confrontation, missile defense would be irrelevant at best. For starters, the probability of a country such as North Korea successfully launching a missile capable of delivering a nuclear warhead to U.S. territory is low. So when all of the uncertainties in missile and warhead performance are added up, the chance of success probably wouldn't be higher than a few percent (which, by the way, is considered a highly potent threat worthy of a multibillion-dollar investment in missile defense). Missile defense eventually might be able to reduce that chance, maybe even considerably, but it will never reduce it to zero. In other words, the defending side would still face a threat that isn't much less credible than it was without missile defense. So the best missile defense can do is to replace one small probability with another. Yet, since nobody knows what exactly these probabilities are in the first place, it would just add one more level of uncertainty to an already uncertain situation without making a fundamental difference.

It's understandable that people often talk about European missile defense as one of the ways in which to deal with the missile threat posed by Iran. Or that someday missile defense could provide insurance for nuclear disarmament—this is the vision that [President] Ronald Reagan had. When framed in this way, missile defense seems like a promising way out of difficult situations. But this promise is false. If a real confrontation ever comes about (and let's hope it never happens), we quickly would find out that missile defense offers no meaningful protection whatsoever.

A Missile Defense System Will Not Defend the United States from a Missile Attack

Lisbeth Gronlund

Lisbeth Gronlund is codirector of the Union of Concerned Scientists' Nuclear Weapons and Global Security program.

As you know, this year [2008] marks the 25th anniversary of President [Ronald] Reagan's famous "Star Wars" speech announcing his plan to develop a missile defense system that would make nuclear weapons "impotent and obsolete." His vision of a "shield that could protect us from nuclear missiles just as a roof protects a family from the rain" was appealing to many people. This was a time when the Soviets and the United States possessed 35,000 and 25,000 nuclear weapons, respectively.

The task now—defending against potential future North Korean or Iranian long-range missiles—is far less demanding than defending against thousands of incoming Soviet missiles.

Antimissile technology has also come a long way in the past 25 years. Guidance and homing have improved so much that all current U.S. missile defense systems use "hit-to-kill" technology intended to destroy the incoming target by ramming into it. Previous defenses against long-range missiles were designed to use nuclear-tipped interceptors to destroy a warhead at a distance.

However, the United States is no closer today to being able to effectively defend against long-range ballistic missiles than it was 25 years ago. . . .

Missile Defense Flaws

The Pentagon has yet to demonstrate that the U.S. Ground-Based [Midcourse] Defense (GMD) system is capable of defending against a long-range ballistic missile in a real-world situation. The tests have demonstrated that the kill vehicle is able to home on and collide with an identifiable target, but under highly scripted conditions. A February 2008 Government Accountability Office report concluded that these tests have been "developmental in nature, and do not provide sufficient realism" to assess the system's potential effectiveness.

There is little or no prospect that the United States will develop a defense system that could defend against real-world long-range missiles in the foreseeable future.

To permit deployment of the fledgling Ground-Based [Midcourse] Defense system, the Missile Defense Agency (MDA) has not followed the normal accounting and testing procedures that apply to all other weapons systems. For example, the system does not comply with the "fly before you buy" law, designed to prevent the military from purchasing weapons that are unsuitable for their real-world mission or do not work as intended. Under this law, a major defense program may not produce more than a small number of weapons—generally for testing purposes—until the Pentagon's director of operational testing and evaluation issues a report stating whether the testing and evaluation was adequate and whether the results show that the weapon system is effective and suitable for combat. That will not be possible until the Pentagon conducts realistic tests, and that may be many years from now, if ever.

To circumvent the rules, the MDA refers to the Ground-Based [Midcourse] Defense components as "fielded" rather than "deployed," and has claimed that they are "test assets" used as part of the test program.

Moreover, there is little or no prospect that the United States will develop a defense system that could defend against real-world long-range missiles in the foreseeable future. As a 2000 Union of Concerned Scientists–Massachusetts Institute of Technology technical report, "Countermeasures," concluded, any country with the capability and motivation to build long-range missiles and fire them at the United States also would have the capability and motivation to equip those missiles with effective countermeasures, such as decoys. That report assessed the National Missile Defense (NMD) system being planned at that time. The NMD system was in principle more capable than the GMD system is, since it included space-based infrared sensors as well as ground-based radars, so the conclusion of the report holds for the GMD system as well.

The availability of countermeasures was also discussed in the September 1999 National Intelligence Estimate on "Foreign Missile Developments and the Ballistic Missile Threat to the United States Through 2015," which stated:

"We assess that countries developing ballistic missiles would also develop various responses to U.S. theater and national defenses. Russia and China each have developed numerous countermeasures and probably are willing to sell the requisite technologies.

"Many countries, such as North Korea, Iran, and Iraq probably would rely initially on readily available technology—including separating RVs [reentry vehicles], spin-stabilized RVs, RV reorientation, radar absorbing material (RAM), booster fragmentation, low-power jammers, chaff, and simple (balloon) decoys—to develop penetration aids and countermeasures.

"These countries could develop countermeasures based on these technologies by the time they flight test their missiles."

These reports make clear that countermeasures pose a fundamental problem for the GMD system at a conceptual level—not just at the technical level. An independent panel should have conducted a big picture review of the program at its inception, but it is not too late for such a review now. The members of such a panel should not be chosen on a partisan basis, but rather for their expertise and independent-mindedness. . . .

As the 1998 [Secretary of Defense Donald] Rumsfeld commission report on the ballistic missile threat emphasized: Absence of evidence is not evidence of absence. It is important to remember that this applies to the development of countermeasures for missiles and not just the missiles themselves.

The Missile Defense Agency has still not addressed the countermeasure problem. In Senate testimony on April 1, [Lt.] General [Trey] Obering stated that MDA "conducted an integrated flight test last September involving a realistic target launched from Alaska." However, the target included no countermeasures; General Obering is apparently defining a "realistic target" as one without countermeasures. General Obering went on to say, "While the [GMD] system is developmental, it is available today to our leadership to meet real-world threats."

If MDA believes the GMD system has the ability to intercept targets with countermeasures, then it should demonstrate this through rigorous testing. Until then, Congress should provide no funding to purchase and deploy additional interceptors or radars.

It is also important that the committee looks into the current testing plans for the GMD system. When does the MDA plan to test against a threat using realistic countermeasures, and what are these countermeasures? When does MDA plan to test against a tumbling warhead? It would also be useful if Congress required MDA to set up an independent red team charged with developing and building simple but realistic countermeasures.

In addition, an independent review panel is also needed to review developments in the GMD system on an ongoing basis. Such a review could examine both past and current issues.

For example, one of the first flyby tests, IFT-1A, was a "proof-of-concept" test intended to demonstrate that the infrared sensors on the kill vehicle could discriminate the warhead from decoys. However, the discrimination algorithm assumed detailed prior knowledge about the characteristics of the warhead and countermeasures—an unwarranted assumption. There have also been other ongoing questions about this test, which this committee and an independent panel should look into as well.

It is dangerous if military and political leaders believe the GMD system is effective. Such misinformation contributes to bad decision making.

A current issue that also merits review by this committee is the capability of the proposed European Midcourse Radar (EMR). On April 1, in discussing long-range Iranian missiles, General Obering testified that the EMR would "provide critical midcourse tracking data on threats launched out of the Middle East." However, recent technical analysis suggests that the radar's range is too short to provide track data or discrimination for long-range missiles launched from the Middle East toward the United States.

The Danger of Misinformed Decision Makers

The pursuit of missile defenses against long-range missiles has been expensive, and entailed significant opportunity costs. However, the greatest costs are the security costs the United States continues to bear.

First, it is dangerous if military and political leaders believe the GMD system is effective. Such misinformation contributes to bad decision making. For example, if decision makers believed that the GMD system could reliably intercept ballistic missiles launched by North Korea, they might be less motivated to pursue diplomatic means to address the North Korean missile program. In a crisis, under the mistaken impression that its missile defenses could reliably stop incoming missiles, U.S. leaders might take actions that make it more likely that an adversary would launch a missile attack.

It is not difficult to find examples in which the perceptions of high-level policy makers differed starkly from the technical assessment of experts who were more familiar with the details of a situation. A striking example is the explosion of the space shuttle *Challenger* in 1986. It is clear in retrospect that the technical experts who understood the space shuttle in detail knew that the unusually cold temperatures on the night of the launch represented a significant risk if the launch proceeded. But this was not understood by the high-level officials who made the decision to launch, and the result was disastrous. Some of these officials were certainly influenced by overstated claims of the shuttle's reliability.

Elevated Threats from Russia and China

Second, as long as the United States and Russia continue to maintain nuclear weapons to deter each other, any U.S. steps to deploy a defense system that Russia believes could intercept a significant number of its survivable long-range missile forces will undermine efforts to reduce nuclear threats. This link between offensive weapons and missile defenses was clearly demonstrated in the 1986 Reykjavik [Iceland] summit meeting, when President [Ronald] Reagan's adherence to missile defense scuttled an opportunity to pursue President Mikhail Gorbachev's offer to negotiate deep cuts in nuclear stockpiles. Ironically, missile defense precluded taking a real step toward achieving Reagan's goal of rendering nuclear weapons obsolete.

Today, the risk of a premeditated Russian or Chinese nuclear attack on the United States is essentially zero. But because Russia continues to maintain more than a thousand nuclear weapons on high alert (as does the United States), ready to be launched within a matter of minutes, there is still a danger of an accidental or unauthorized attack, or of a mistaken launch in response to a false warning. Indeed, such attacks are the only military threats that could destroy the United States as a functioning society.

Russia's incentive to maintain its weapons on alert would be strengthened if it believed the United States was deploying a system that could threaten its ability to retaliate. In fact, when the United States was trying to renegotiate the terms of the ABM [Anti-Ballistic Missile] Treaty in the late 1990s, it argued that Russia need not fear a U.S. defense system as long as it kept its missiles on high alert.

China, meanwhile, has a very small arsenal of roughly 20 long-range missiles that it relies on for deterrence. However, it could decide to offset U.S. defense deployments by increasing its arsenal, which could in turn prompt India and then Pakistan to increase their nuclear arsenals.

On one level, the United States is aware of this linkage. It has stressed that its Ground-Based [Midcourse] Defense system is intended to protect against potential future threats from developing countries, and has stated that deployments would be "limited" so that Russia and China would not see them as a threat to their nuclear deterrents. However, from Russia's and China's perspective, the issue is whether U.S. actions match its words.

In the coming years, the United States plans to increase the number of interceptors that are capable—at least in principle—of defending against long-range missiles. Congress has allocated funds for 40 Ground-Based [Midcourse] Defense interceptors, to be deployed in Alaska and California. The United States is negotiating with Poland and the Czech Republic to deploy an additional 10 Ground-Based [Midcourse] Defense interceptors and one or two radars in Europe near the Russian border. Russia has strongly objected to this plan.

Within five years, the United States also is slated to deploy some 150 interceptor missiles on 18 ships as part of its Aegis missile defense system, which is designed to defend against intermediate-range ballistic missiles. However, the United States plans to produce an upgraded version of the interceptor to allow the Aegis system to defend against long-range missiles as well. Thus, Russia and China may worry that they could soon face some 200 U.S. interceptors designed to destroy long-range missiles.

Compared with China's 20 long-range nuclear-armed missiles, 200 interceptors constitute a relatively large deployment. While Russia has a far larger arsenal, it may assume that most of it would be destroyed by a U.S. first strike. While the scientists in these countries may understand that these interceptors can be defeated by straightforward countermeasures, worst-case analyses by political and military leaders, as well as a desire to have a visible response for both domestic and international audiences, may prompt both China and Russia to build or retain larger nuclear forces than they otherwise would, and may lead Russia to retain its missiles on high alert. . . .

In summary, the GMD program offers no prospect of defending the United States from a real-world missile attack and undermines efforts to eliminate the real nuclear threats to the United States.

CHAPTER 4

Is the US Response to the Nuclear Weapons Threat Adequate?

Chapter Overview

Kingston Reif and Chad O'Carroll

Kingston Reif is the director of nuclear nonproliferation at the Center for Arms Control and Non-Proliferation, where his work focuses on arms control, nuclear nonproliferation, nuclear weapons, and preventing nuclear terrorism. Chad O'Carroll is a graduate student studying nonproliferation and international security at King's College in London.

The fiscal year 2008 National Defense Authorization Act mandated the U.S. Department of Defense to undertake a Nuclear Posture Review [NPR], a comprehensive review of U.S. nuclear weapons strategy and policy for the next five to ten years. The review, which began in the spring of 2009, was originally scheduled to be submitted to Congress in December 2009, but it has been delayed until March or April 2010.

The 2010 Nuclear Posture Review marks the third such comprehensive study since the end of the Cold War. The first was completed by the [Bill] Clinton administration in 1994 and the second by the George W. Bush administration in 2002. While the 1994 and 2002 reviews were classified, the current study will produce an unclassified report as one of its products.

Purpose of the Nuclear Posture Review

President [Barack] Obama's April 5, 2009, speech in Prague presenting a vision of a world without nuclear weapons provides the backdrop for the NPR. The review will attempt to strike a balance between the president's pledge to reduce the role and number of nuclear weapons and his commitment to maintaining a safe, secure, and effective nuclear stockpile so long as nuclear weapons exist.

Kingston Reif and Chad O'Carroll, "The 2010 U.S. Nuclear Posture Review," armscontrolcenter.org, 2010. Copyright © 2010 by Center for Arms Control and Non-Proliferation. All rights reserved. Reproduced by permission.

Specifically, the review will weigh in on such important issues as:

- the role and purpose of the U.S. nuclear arsenal

- the appropriate number, types, and composition of U.S. nuclear warheads and delivery vehicles (i.e., the missiles and bombers used to deliver nuclear warheads to their targets) necessary to meet the designated role and purpose

- the resources and facilities required to maintain a U.S. nuclear arsenal

- preventing the spread of nuclear weapons and know-how to additional states and terrorists

---

The [Nuclear Posture] Review seems ready to make the prevention of nuclear terrorism a goal equal to the traditional objectives of preventing . . . state-led nuclear weapons development and usage.

Significance of the Nuclear Posture Review

The Nuclear Posture Review will influence the implementation of the president's agenda to reduce the role and number of nuclear weapons laid out in Prague. This agenda includes pursuit of a follow-on agreement to the Strategic Arms Reduction Treaty (START), which expired on December 5, 2009, ratification of the Comprehensive [Nuclear-]Test-Ban Treaty (CTBT), safeguarding and eliminating all vulnerable nuclear materials worldwide within four years, a Fissile Material Cut-Off Treaty (FMCT) to ban the production of highly enriched uranium and plutonium for weapons purposes, and a successful Nuclear Non-Proliferation Treaty Review Conference in 2010.

Since ratification of the START follow-on agreement seems unlikely in the first half of 2010, the Nuclear Posture Review will be one of the—if not the—principal U.S. actions completed before the Nuclear Non-Proliferation Treaty Review Conference begins in May 2010. A review that does not depart from the status quo could contribute to a perception among the nonnuclear weapon states that the nuclear weapon states are not living up to the basic bargain of the treaty. This could in turn make the nonnuclear weapons states reluctant to approve further nonproliferation measures, such as enhanced inspection protocols or support for tougher measures against Iran and North Korea.

Though not yet fully completed, some of the early results of the review have already had an impact on U.S. nuclear policy and planning. Some examples include:

- The early work on the review established the direction of the START follow-on negotiations with Russia. In testimony to the Senate Armed Services Committee on July 9, 2009, General James Cartwright, vice chairman of the Joint Chiefs of Staff, said: "We prioritized in the Nuclear Posture Review . . . the activities and the analysis that would be necessary to support the time lines associated with . . . the follow-on START negotiations."

- The review has delivered an early verdict on the president's pledge in Prague to maintain a safe, secure, and effective nuclear stockpile so long as nuclear weapons exist. Deputy Secretary of Energy Dan Poneman stated in a February 17, 2010, speech that "the early analysis from the Nuclear Posture Review concluded that providing that assurance, especially at lower numbers of nuclear weapons, will require increased investments to strengthen an aging physical infrastructure and to sustain scientific and technical talent at our nation's national security laboratories." The Obama administration's fiscal year 2011 budget request, which was released on February 1, 2010, devotes $7 billion for maintaining the U.S. nuclear stockpile and complex, and for related science and technology programs, an increase of $600 million over what Congress appropriated last year.

Other tentative results of the review have begun to emerge:

- In keeping with President Obama's elevation of nuclear terrorism as the principal threat to U.S. national security, the review seems ready to make the prevention of nuclear terrorism a goal equal to the traditional objectives of preventing both state-led nuclear weapons development and usage.

- The review appears poised to call for the retirement of the Tomahawk land-attack missile, a sea-launched cruise missile that during the Cold War was deployed on some U.S. attack submarines but has remained in storage at military bases on the U.S. mainland since the early 1990s.

Preparation for the Nuclear Posture Review

According to a June 2009 Department of Defense terms of reference fact sheet, the review was being conducted simultaneously with the Quadrennial Defense Review (released on February 1, 2010), the Ballistic Missile Defense Review (released on February 1, 2010), the Space [Posture] Review, the START follow-on negotiations, and preparations for the 2010 Nuclear Non-Proliferation Treaty Review Conference.

The Nuclear Posture Review has been led by the Office of the Secretary of Defense and Joint Staff, in consultation with the secretary of energy and secretary of state. Primary responsibility has resided with the Under Secretary of Defense for Policy Michèle Flournoy and the Vice Chairman of the Joint Chiefs of Staff Gen. Cartwright.

The process has embraced a "whole of government" approach, meaning that the Department of Defense has consulted with other government departments and agencies, congressional committees, and even nuclear scholars from think tanks, advocacy organizations, and academia. The results of the review will guide nuclear policy across the entire U.S. foreign policy–making apparatus.

Key Challenges

Recent reports have indicated that there was a lack of consensus among the participants in the review process on the future direction of U.S. nuclear policy. The release of the review was delayed from December 2009 to February 2010 and then again to sometime in March or April 2010 because many of the key issues had yet to be resolved or approved.

Some argue that the U.S. should . . . declare that [it] will never use nuclear weapons first, but only in response to a nuclear attack.

Some of these issues have included:

The role and purpose of the U.S. nuclear arsenal

Since the end of the Cold War the United States has maintained a policy of "calculated ambiguity" regarding when it might use nuclear weapons. According to this policy, nuclear weapons are necessary to "provide credible military options to deter a wide range of threats, including WMD [weapons of mass destruction] and large-scale conventional military force."

At issue is whether the U.S. should retain the current policy of calculated ambiguity or revise it in favor of something that is more in keeping with the objectives laid out by President Obama in Prague. One popular formulation is that the review should state that the sole purpose of nuclear weapons is to deter nuclear attacks on the U.S. and its allies. Some argue that the U.S. should be even more explicit and declare that the U.S. will never use nuclear weapons first, but only in response to a nuclear attack.

The appropriate number of nuclear weapons

As noted above, the Nuclear Posture Review has been closely coordinated with the START follow-on negotiations to inform the U.S. negotiating position. The early results of the review were reflected in the "Joint Understanding for the START Follow-On Treaty" agreed to by President Obama and [Russian President Dmitry] Medvedev in Moscow in July 2009. The joint understanding stated that the START follow-on agreement will limit the U.S. and Russia to 1,500–1,675 operationally deployed strategic warheads and 500–1,100 strategic delivery vehicles.

At issue is whether the U.S. can undertake even more significant reductions with Russia in the future. One view is that if the U.S. were to limit the purpose of nuclear weapons to deterring nuclear attacks on the U.S. and its allies, it could reduce the size of its nuclear arsenal far below the levels outlined in the joint understanding. Others argue that such dramatic reductions could undermine the confidence of U.S. allies in the credibility of the U.S. nuclear deterrent, thereby encouraging them to develop their own nuclear arsenals, and invite peer competition from smaller nuclear powers such as China.

Related to the total number of U.S. nuclear weapons is the number of nuclear weapons deployed in Europe. It is estimated that the U.S. deploys approximately 200 B61 gravity bombs at six bases in Italy, Turkey, Belgium, Germany, and the Netherlands.

The review could call for the beginning of consultations with NATO [North Atlantic Treaty Organization] to ultimately withdraw—or at the very least consolidate—the remaining U.S. nuclear weapons in Europe. A passage in the 2010 Quadrennial Defense Review stated that the Nuclear Posture Review will outline "new, tailored, regional deterrence architectures" which will "make possible a reduced role for nuclear weapons in our national security strategy." On February 19, 2010, a spokesperson for the Belgian prime minister proclaimed that Belgium, Germany, Luxembourg, the Netherlands, and Norway intend to demand within NATO "that nuclear arms on European soil belonging to other NATO member states are removed." According to one commentator, "presumably, some coordination with Washington has taken place [regarding the statement]."

Maintaining U.S. nuclear warheads

Since announcing a moratorium on nuclear testing in 1992, the U.S. has opted to maintain its existing arsenal of nuclear warheads through stockpile stewardship and life extension (also known as refurbishment). This has involved replacing aging, mostly nonnuclear components with parts that hew as closely as possible to the original design specifications. Some claim that selective parts replacement cannot extend the life of the existing arsenal indefinitely and that new warhead designs may be necessary to achieve President Obama's pledge to maintain a safe, secure, and effective nuclear stockpile so long as nuclear weapons exist.

Not only will the Nuclear Posture Review determine U.S. nuclear weapons policy for the next decade, but it could also influence the attitudes of other states toward nuclear weapons.

However, a September 2009 report by the JASON defense advisory group concluded that "lifetimes of today's nuclear warheads could be extended for decades, with no anticipated loss in confidence." The bipartisan Congressional Commission on the Strategic Posture of the United States noted in its final report that existing life extension programs and new warhead designs represent opposite ends of a spectrum of options to maintain the arsenal. Others argue that new warhead designs could undermine U.S. nonproliferation objectives by encouraging other states to build new and more advanced nuclear arsenals.

In September 2009 Under Secretary of State for Arms Control and International Security Ellen Tauscher stated that the Nuclear Posture Review would not revive the now defunct Reliable Replacement Warhead program. Yet some observers point out that the Nuclear Posture Review could recommend making extensive changes to warheads—or even new warhead designs—under the auspices of the newly created stockpile management program.

Transforming the Status Quo

The Nuclear Posture Review's recommendations will likely echo the many different voices that contributed to the review process. If the 2010 NPR does attempt to please all of its many authors, it will likely fall well short of President Obama's transformational vision.

Not only will the Nuclear Posture Review determine U.S. nuclear weapons policy for the next decade, but it could also influence the attitudes of other states toward nuclear weapons. Reports indicate that the White House has instructed the Pentagon to present the president with options that reflect the transformational agenda he laid out in Prague. Continued presidential involvement and attention will be required to ensure that the NPR does not merely perpetuate the status quo.

Changes to US Nuclear Policy Offer Steps Toward a Nonnuclear World

George Perkovich

George Perkovich is vice president for studies and director of the Nuclear Policy Program at Carnegie Endowment for International Peace.

The [Barack] Obama administration released a new nuclear arms strategy on Tuesday [April 6, 2010]. The Nuclear Posture Review [NPR] narrows the use of nuclear weapons and says that the primary role of the U.S. nuclear posture is to deter an attack on the United States and prevent nuclear proliferation and terrorism. . . .

What Is the Nuclear Posture Review and How Important Is It?

The Nuclear Posture Review [NPR] is a document required by the U.S. Congress, where the secretary of defense sends to Congress the administration's overall view of nuclear weapons—the role that nuclear weapons play in U.S. national security policy, what they want to communicate to allies that we try to reassure with these weapons, and how they communicate to potential adversaries of the United States what the deterrent strategy of the United States is.

From that document then come instructions which the military uses to actually design the targeting options for nuclear weapons and the planning of the U.S. nuclear force posture. The posture review also in a sense sets out the requirements for nuclear weapons, which then has implications in the budgets of the Department of Energy, the Department of Defense, and has implications for the size of the infrastructure necessary to produce and maintain U.S. nuclear weapons.

So it's your kind of basic operating system for nuclear weapons.

This posture review reflects what the military understands, which is that it's almost impossible to imagine a circumstance . . . where the United States would threaten to use nuclear weapons.

What Are the Key Elements of the New Report?

The new posture review departs from the one that the [George W.] Bush administration did early in its term in several ways. One, the Obama one says that the primary objective or concern of U.S. nuclear posture is to prevent the proliferation of nuclear weapons to other states and to prevent the use of nuclear weapons by terrorists. This is interesting because past administrations have said these are very important things, but it's not part of our nuclear policy and our nuclear posture.

The administration also says very clearly that the goal of the United States is ultimately to have a world without nuclear weapons and acknowledges we're far from that possibility today, but that it is an objective and therefore that the United States will try to lead the world in reducing the role of nuclear weapons in everyone's national security policy.

So, the United States would try to lead by example and, as much as possible, to reduce reliance on nuclear weapons in U.S. security, but also to then encourage and put pressure on others to do the same.

So those are two kinds of interesting changes in priority, in a sense, of this posture.

How Significantly Did President Obama Alter U.S. Nuclear Strategy?

Actually, the Bush administration got an unfair criticism. People around the world didn't like the administration for a lot of reasons, and they basically interpreted the Bush administration's strategy as somehow increasing the reliance by the United States on nuclear weapons and lowering the threshold that would decide whether the United States would use nuclear weapons. Neither of those was true.

The Bush administration also sought to reduce the role of nuclear weapons, and I would argue that the Obama posture review extends what was already a process begun by the Bush administration and it extends it in ways reflecting the realities of the world.

The United States has greater conventional, nonnuclear military capabilities. It's fought a couple of wars since the last posture review in Iraq and Afghanistan. These are major wars, cost more than a trillion dollars, and it's obvious to everyone that we would never use nuclear weapons in these situations. They're irrelevant, basically, and we have lots of other needs that need to be concentrated upon and fulfilled.

And so, this posture review reflects what the military understands, which is that it's almost impossible to imagine a circumstance—other than a nuclear attack by a major state against the United States—where the United States would threaten to use nuclear weapons and so we ought to have a policy that reflects that reality.

Does the New Policy Limit America's Nuclear Deterrent?

If you ask, how would the United States interpret it if a competitor makes declarations about its nuclear posture. Let's say Russia for example. If the Russians came out and said, "Americans trust us, we won't use nuclear weapons against you."

Do you think the U.S. government, Congress, and the military are just going to take that at face value and say well the Russians said they won't use nuclear weapons against us therefore let's forget about the thousands of nuclear weapons that they have. No. You want to look at what their capabilities are, you want to look at scenarios—you want to be real.

The United States is not going to get rid of its nuclear weapons alone. . . . As long as others have weapons, the United States will have to retain them.

Similarly, what the United States actually says in terms of whether or not it's beating its chest and saying to the world out there, don't you dare do anything to us or we will nuke you. That they would take that seriously and as gospel is strange credulity. But similarly if we said to our potential adversaries, don't worry we're past nuclear weapons. We still have a couple thousand of them, but don't worry we're nice guys. They won't believe that either.

What they are looking at is what capabilities you have, the scenarios they can imagine of conflict, and the basic reality that if the United States was threatened in a fundamental way, its existence was threatened, an extreme threat or one of its allies like Japan was threatened that way, the other guy knows that if we have nuclear weapons and that's the only thing we can use to defeat the other guy, that's what we're going to do.

So it doesn't matter so much what we say about it, it's that capability and that context that will determine whether a state is deterred or not.

How Does the NPR Relate to Obama's Goal of Moving Toward a World Without Nuclear Weapons?

This posture review states in many places that the goal of the United States is to move toward a world without nuclear weapons. It's not unilateral, the United States is not going to get rid of its nuclear weapons alone. And it states clearly that as long as others have weapons, the United States will have to retain them and we will have to retain them in a safe and reliable manner.

But it does commit to this goal. It says if others want to work with us, we're prepared to go there. It very specifically, for example, invites Russia and China—the two main potential competitors of the United States in a nuclear sphere—to further strategic dialogue, to further develop common understanding, so we can avoid any offensive nuclear competition, but actually move to reduce the role of these weapons in each of our cases. And to make sure that we have stable relations so that we don't get into a crisis that could lead to a nuclear war or the threat of a nuclear war.

So that's very important in the posture, that invitation to Russia and China to reduce the role of nuclear weapons.

Why Is the Strategy Controversial?

I don't think this is going to be controversial. There may be people on the Far Right who don't like it, but in many cases they don't understand reality, whether it was under the Bush administration or any previous administration. If you don't understand the reality that, since 1945, we haven't used nuclear weapons, no one has used nuclear weapons in anger, that every president has understood that this is a taboo that they don't want to cross and that we don't make nuclear threats idly. You have to understand that and many people don't.

You also have to understand that the U.S. military doesn't want to use nuclear weapons, doesn't feel that it would need to use nuclear weapons, and that we have enough conventional military capabilities to deter any rational actor from threatening us. The statements in this posture review don't really change all of that. There is some reassurance to adversaries, but it's not the United States unilaterally giving up military power.

On the left, it will be criticized because they will argue that the president doesn't go far enough to say that the only purpose for nuclear weapons is to deter the use of nuclear weapons by others.

So the posture review says, look we want to move to that point of saying the only way in which we would consider using nuclear weapons is to retaliate to a nuclear attack. But states may develop biological weapon capabilities in the future and so we may then face a massive threat that is nonnuclear and so we would reserve this option. And more importantly today, we have some allies that we care greatly about, including South Korea, who worry that they face an adversary, in this case North Korea, that could threaten them with massive artillery attacks because the distance between Seoul and North Korea is very slight.

And our ally South Korea might want us to still threaten North Korea with a nuclear response even though North Korea would be attacking South Korea conventionally. The U.S. military knows that we can defeat North Korea without nuclear weapons, but in order to reassure our ally South Korea we're not saying it quite that way. We're leaving the options fuzzier because this is reassuring to our ally South Korea.

Are Disarmament Advocates Going to Be Disappointed by the NPR?

Some of the disarmament advocates around the world might be disappointed because people wanted President Obama to have a posture and declare that the only purpose is to deter the use of nuclear weapons by others.

It's very important to realize that this is the best posture review that the president and his administration thought could get the 67 votes in the U.S. Senate needed to ratify the START [Strategic Arms Reduction Treaty] treaty.

On the one hand, you could have a posture review which says lovely things opposed to nuclear weapons that the disarmament community would applaud, but would in turn reduce the chances you could actually get a real treaty to reduce nuclear weapons ratified in the Senate.

So the administration decided to have a posture review that is conceived in terms of what we need to do to get votes in the Senate to actually implement reductions that can lead toward the future that disarmament advocates might want, even if our language now may disappoint them.

How Does the NPR Set the Stage for International Policies?

The NPR is very important—it's a document that will guide U.S. policy for the next five years. The new START treaty which will be signed in Prague on April 8 hopefully ratified this year was already informed by the Nuclear Posture Review.

When the Nuclear Posture Review was being drafted, the negotiators of the START treaty and the Pentagon and the military got together and said, here's the basic parameters of what we're going to talk about in START, in the Nuclear Posture Review that you are doing, do you have any problem with us reducing to these levels. And the answer was no, we can maintain deterrence, the security of the United States is ensured at the levels that we are talking about with START. So in a way the posture review came before the START treaty even though it's being announced only two days before the signing of the treaty.

Politically what all this means is that the president's agenda that he announced a year ago in Prague of reducing the role of nuclear weapons now has the posture review which does that, the START treaty coming several days later which demonstrates it, the Nuclear Security Summit in Washington on April 12–13 with the heads of more than 40 countries showing a commitment to try to keep nuclear material from terrorists (that's the focus of the Nuclear Security Summit).

All of which is meant to give momentum and show the seriousness of the United States as the review conference happens in May in New York with all the states in the nonproliferation treaty. So the United States is trying to say look, let's keep the bargain where all of the rest of the world agrees not to get nuclear weapons and to work with us to keep nuclear weapons from terrorists and other states, because we are keeping our side of the bargain. We are doing everything we can to reduce the role of nuclear weapons and reduce the number of nuclear weapons. . . .

Does the New Strategy Influence How the U.S. Can Contain Iran's Nuclear Ambitions?

The NPR is not directed against Iran in any way. If you ask the U.S. military, we don't need nuclear weapons to fight or deter Iran from committing the kind of aggression that militaries prevent. And even if Iran had a handful of nuclear weapons, the United States for the next decade at least is going to have thousands of strategic nuclear weapons as well as hundreds of shorter range nuclear weapons.

There is no nuclear equation with Iran, and the U.S. military knows that even if people in the public or Congress say we may need to nuke Iran. That is not the way the military thinks about it.

What the posture review can help do though is encourage other countries to work with us to isolate Iran diplomatically, politically, and economically, with an understanding that the United States is trying to be progressive or constructive in the way the rest of the world thinks about nuclear weapons.

And therefore we strengthen our persuasiveness in getting the rest of the world to be constructive with us as we deal with the kind of threats that Iran poses.

Changes to US Nuclear Strategy Are Largely Meaningless

Stephen M. Walt

Stephen M. Walt is a professor of international affairs at Harvard University's John F. Kennedy School of Government.

The [Barack] Obama administration is now rolling out the results of its "Nuclear Posture Review [NPR]," and presenting it as a significant if not quite revolutionary rethinking of U.S. nuclear strategy. I haven't seen the full text of the document and have only excerpts and press reports to go by, but the basic idea is to narrow the range of scenarios in which the United States would threaten a nuclear response.

To be a bit more specific, instead of reserving the option of nuclear strikes in response to a nuclear attack, an attack by other forms of WMD [weapons of mass destruction] (such as biological weapons) or even a large-scale conventional invasion, the review declares that the "fundamental role" of the U.S. arsenal is to deter nuclear attacks on the U.S., its allies, or partners. Accordingly, as a matter of declaratory policy, the review declares that "the United States will not use or threaten to use nuclear weapons against non-nuclear weapons states that are party to the Nuclear Non-Proliferation Treaty [NPT, the Treaty on the Non-Proliferation of Nuclear Weapons] and in compliance with their nuclear non-proliferation obligations."

The exceptions to this narrower focus would be nonnuclear attacks by any nuclear-armed state, or states that the United

States deems to be in violation of the NPT translation: We still reserve the option of first nuclear use against Iran and North Korea.

A Meaningless NPT

Lots of ink will no doubt be spilled analyzing this shift in declaratory policy, and nuclear theologians will spend time at conferences and workshops parsing the fine-grained implications of the change. And stay tuned for assorted hawkish windbags and right-wing think-tankers declaring that this new language has somehow imperiled U.S. security, even though we still have thousands of nuclear weapons in our arsenal and the strongest conventional forces in the world.

I'll concede that this new statement may have some public relations value—i.e, it lowers the priority given to nuclear weapons in U.S. strategic thinking, consistent with Obama's commitment to eventually reduce global nuclear arsenals. But from a purely strategic perspective, this new statement is largely meaningless. To the extent that it does matter, it may even be counterproductive.

Here's why. No matter what the U.S. government *says* about its nuclear strategy, no potential adversary can confidently assume that the U.S. would stick to its declared policy in the event of a crisis or war. If you were a world leader thinking about launching a major conventional attack on an important U.S. ally or interest, or contemplating the use of chemical or biological weapons in a situation where the United States was involved, would *you* conclude that it was safe to do so simply because Barack Obama said back in 2010 that the U.S. wasn't going to use nuclear weapons in that situation?

Of course you wouldn't, because there is absolutely nothing to stop the United States from changing its mind. You'd worry that the United States might conclude that the interests at stake were worth issuing a nuclear threat, and maybe even using a nuclear weapon, and that it really didn't matter what anyone had said in a posture review or an interview with a few journalists. And you'd also have to worry that the situation might escalate in unpredictable or unintended ways—what [foreign affairs professor] Thomas Schelling famously termed the "threat that leaves something to chance"—and thereby ruin your whole day.

To the extent that nuclear weapons deter—and I happen to think they do—it is the mere fact of their existence and not the specific words we use when we speak about them. In short, nobody can know for certain if, when or how a nuclear state might actually use its arsenal to protect its interests, and that goes for any potential aggressor too. Because the prospect of nuclear use is so awful, no minimally rational aggressor is going to run that risk solely because of some words typed in a posture statement.

Motivating Iran to Pursue Nuclear Weapons

Furthermore, the decision to exclude nuclear weapons states, non-signatories of the NPT, or states we deem in violation of it (e.g., Iran) strikes me as both too clever by half and maybe counterproductive. The purpose seems to be to give these states an additional incentive to sign the NPT or to conform to it, but it's hard to believe that this statement will have that effect on anyone. India, Pakistan and Israel are all non-signatories, but surely they aren't worried about U.S. "first use" against them and so this statement will be irrelevant to their nuclear calculations.

The real target of this exception is Iran (and conceivably North Korea and Syria). At best, this new statement will have little or no effect, for the reasons noted above (i.e., no one knows what we might do in a crisis or war, so pledges of no-first-use are essentially meaningless). At worst, however, excluding Iran in this fashion—which amounts to saying that Iran is still a nuclear target even when it has no weapons of its own—merely gives them additional incentives to pursue a nuclear weapons option. In particular, declaring that we reserve the right of "first use" against Iran *now* (when it has no weapons at all), sounds like a good way to convince them that their own deterrent might be a pretty nice thing to have.

Remarkably, U.S. policy makers never seem to realize that the same arguments they use to justify our own nuclear arsenal apply even more powerfully to states whose security is a lot more precarious than America's. If the U.S. government believes that "the fundamental role" of U.S. nuclear weapons is to deter nuclear attacks on the United States, and the United States is now proclaiming that it still reserves the option of using nuclear weapons *first* against nonnuclear Iran (under some admittedly extreme circumstances), then wouldn't a sensible Iranian leadership conclude that it could use a nuclear arsenal of its own, whose "fundamental role" would be to deter us from doing just that?

Changes in Nuclear Strategy Fail to Defend the United States

Charles Krauthammer

Charles Krauthammer is a syndicated columnist and political commentator who writes for the Washington Post's *op-ed page.*

Nuclear doctrine consists of thinking the unthinkable. It involves making threats and promising retaliation that is cruel and destructive beyond imagining. But it has its purpose: to prevent war in the first place.

During the Cold War, we let the Russians know that if they dared use their huge conventional military advantage and invaded Western Europe, they risked massive U.S. nuclear retaliation. Goodbye Moscow.

Was this credible? Would we have done it? Who knows? No one's ever been there. A nuclear posture is just that—a declaratory policy designed to make the other guy think twice.

Our policies did. The result was called deterrence. For half a century, it held. The Soviets never invaded. We never used nukes. That's why nuclear doctrine is important.

A Naive Nuclear Policy

The [Barack] Obama administration has just issued a new one that "includes significant changes to the U.S. nuclear posture," said Defense Secretary Bob Gates. First among these involves the U.S. response to being attacked with biological or chemical weapons.

Under the old doctrine, supported by every president of both parties for decades, any aggressor ran the risk of a cataclysmic U.S. nuclear response that would leave the attacking nation a cinder and a memory.

Again: Credible? Doable? No one knows. But the threat was very effective.

Under President Obama's new policy, however, if the state that has just attacked us with biological or chemical weapons is "in compliance with the [Nuclear] Non-Proliferation Treaty (NPT) [also known as the Treaty on the Non-Proliferation of Nuclear Weapons]," explained Gates, then "the U.S. pledges not to use or threaten to use nuclear weapons against it."

Imagine the scenario: Hundreds of thousands are lying dead in the streets of Boston after a massive anthrax or nerve gas attack. The president immediately calls in the lawyers to determine whether the attacking state is in compliance with the NPT. If it turns out that the attacker is up to date with its latest IAEA [International Atomic Energy Agency] inspections, well, it gets immunity from nuclear retaliation. (Our response is then restricted to bullets, bombs and other conventional munitions.)

However, if the lawyers tell the president that the attacking state is NPT noncompliant, we are free to blow the bastards to nuclear kingdom come.

This is quite insane. It's like saying that if a terrorist deliberately uses his car to mow down a hundred people waiting at a bus stop, the decision as to whether he gets (a) hanged or (b) 100 hours of community service hinges entirely on whether his car had passed emissions inspections.

Apart from being morally bizarre, the Obama policy is strategically loopy. Does anyone believe that North Korea or Iran will be more persuaded to abjure nuclear weapons because they could then carry out a biological or chemical attack on the U.S. without fear of nuclear retaliation?

The naïveté is stunning. Similarly the Obama pledge to forswear development of any new nuclear warheads, indeed, to permit no replacement of aging nuclear components without the authorization of the president himself. This under the theory that our moral example will move other countries to eschew nukes.

[The new U.S. nuclear posture] is deeply worrying to many small nations who for half a century relied on the extended U.S. nuclear umbrella.

On the contrary. The last quarter-century—the time of greatest superpower nuclear arms reduction—is precisely when Iran and North Korea went hell bent into the development of nuclear weapons.

It gets worse. The administration's Nuclear Posture Review declares U.S. determination to "continue to reduce the role of nuclear weapons in deterring non-nuclear attacks." The ultimate aim is to get to a blanket doctrine of no first use.

Encouraging Proliferation

This is deeply worrying to many small nations who for half a century relied on the extended U.S. nuclear umbrella to keep them from being attacked or overrun by far more powerful neighbors. When smaller allies see the United States determined to move inexorably away from that posture—and for them it's not posture, but existential protection—what are they to think?

Fend for yourself. Get yourself your own WMDs [weapons of mass destruction]. Go nuclear if you have to. Do you imagine they are not thinking that in the Persian Gulf?

This administration seems to believe that by restricting retaliatory threats and by downplaying our reliance on nuclear weapons, it is discouraging proliferation.

But the opposite is true. Since World War II, smaller countries have agreed to forgo the acquisition of deterrent forces—nuclear, biological and chemical—precisely because they placed their trust in the firmness, power and reliability of the American deterrent.

Seeing America retreat, they will rethink. And some will arm. There is no greater spur to hyper-proliferation than the furling of the American nuclear umbrella.

A New START Treaty with Russia Will Strengthen US National Security

Jeanne Shaheen

Jeanne Shaheen is a Democratic senator from New Hampshire.

This week [September 2010], the Senate Foreign Relations Committee is scheduled to vote on ratification of the New START [Strategic Arms Reduction Treaty] treaty. From the beginning of our deliberation, committee members have sought to answer the question Defense Secretary Robert Gates posed early in this process: Is the U.S. better off with this treaty or without it?

After a careful and thorough examination, including 12 open and classified hearings, more than 20 expert hearing witnesses, and overwhelming support from across the political spectrum—including the unanimous support of America's military leadership—it is clear that America will be safer and more secure with this treaty than without it. The New START treaty will strengthen our country's national security, and a failure to ratify this treaty could lead to serious consequences as we work to protect our country from the threat of nuclear proliferation.

A Step Forward

Since the end of the Cold War, the nuclear threat facing our country has evolved. The danger of a nuclear exchange between the world's two superpowers has subsided, but the possibility of nuclear weapons falling into the wrong hands has increased. We should not be blind to the catastrophic consequences that nuclear terrorism presents to our world. The New START treaty represents a step forward in avoiding that nuclear nightmare.

Together, the U.S. and Russia account for more than 90 percent of the world's nuclear weapons: an arsenal capable of incalculable damage. As global leaders of the nuclear nonproliferation regime, it is our solemn responsibility to ensure that these weapons and materials do not fall into the wrong hands.

If we are to curb the threat of proliferation and build support in the international community to meet this challenge, we will need to demonstrate to the world that our two nations are serious about responsive and verifiable reductions in our nuclear arsenals. The New START treaty accomplishes this objective by limiting the strategic nuclear forces of the U.S. and Russia. If ratified, the treaty will go far in meeting our ongoing commitments under the Nuclear Non-Proliferation Treaty (NPT) [also known as the Treaty on the Non-Proliferation of Nuclear Weapons] and gives us added credibility to leverage all NPT members to meet their own obligations and commitments.

In addition to limiting the number of strategically deployed weapons, the New START treaty could serve as the foundation for future negotiations on reducing the number of tactical nuclear weapons that experts say pose a potential proliferation threat. As a number of witnesses testified, agreement with Russia on tactical nuclear weapons will be much more difficult—if not impossible—without ratification of the New START treaty.

In addition, the New START treaty will advance U.S. national security by maintaining a credible deterrent for the U.S. and our allies and by guaranteeing verifiable reductions in the numbers of nuclear weapons aimed at our homeland. This is why seven former commanders of U.S. Strategic Command (STRATCOM) wrote to the Senate in July urging the treaty's ratification saying that New START "will enhance American national security."

The New START treaty will give us important insight into the Russian nuclear arsenal. We have now gone more than 280 days without critical intelligence we receive from an on-site verification and monitoring presence in Russia. With the expiration of the original START treaty in December 2009, U.S. inspectors lost access to dozens of Russian sites. If we don't ratify the New START treaty, we will lose this critical information. As outgoing STRATCOM Commander General Kevin Chilton testified, "If we don't get the treaty, [the Russians] are not constrained in their development of force structure and . . . we have no insight into what they're doing. So it's the worst of both possible worlds." In other words, failing to ratify the treaty will put American national security at risk.

The Senate Should Ratify START

Failure to ratify the treaty would also send a dangerous message to Russia and the rest of the world that the U.S. is abandoning the high ground with respect to nuclear reductions. Reversing decades of arms control policy would signal to the world that the U.S. no longer stands behind its nuclear commitments and would undermine the basis for our current global nonproliferation regime.

Arms control has a long history of strong bipartisan support in the Senate. Previous generations of Senate leaders did not allow politics to get in the way of national security. The threat posed by nuclear terrorism, the proliferation of nuclear materials, and a lack of transparency and access to Russia's nuclear program is too dangerous to delay action any further. We must do our part to help build a culture of nuclear accountability and transparency. New START provides that foundation, and the treaty deserves the Senate's ratification this year.

The New START Treaty with Russia Weakens US National Security

Jim DeMint

Jim DeMint is a Republican senator from South Carolina.

The concessions President [Barack] Obama made to Russia to get the New START [Strategic Arms Reduction Treaty] signed are precisely why the Senate should not ratify it.

Giving Russia the Advantage

New START is another Obama giveaway at the expense of U.S. citizens. The treaty mandates strategic nuclear weapons parity with the progeny of an old Cold War foe, yet allows the Russians to maintain a 10-to-1 tactical nuclear-weapons advantage. Whether in warhead and launcher limits, verification, or missile defense, America loses. The treaty dampens the U.S. ability to defend against missile attacks and makes America and her allies vulnerable to rogue nations while receiving nothing for our concessions.

The Obama administration champions the fact that the treaty would limit both countries to 1,550 deployed strategic nuclear warheads each. But Russia could maintain its huge stockpile of roughly 4,000 tactical nuclear weapons, thousands more than the United States has, because the treaty doesn't restrict those types, which can also be affixed to rockets, submarines, and attack aircraft.

The treaty's delivery vehicle limit is also troubling. While U.S. land-based missiles only have one warhead each, the Russians use multiple independent reentry vehicles per missile. Though this is more unstable, it means the Russians can hit

Jim DeMint, "The New START Treaty Weakens U.S. National Security," politics.usnews .com, August 16, 2010. Reproduced by permission.

more targets with fewer launchers. To add insult to injury, launchers carrying nonnuclear, conventional weapons that have the capability to carry a nuclear weapon would count toward this limit as well. This is another win for the Russians: We depend on our conventional weapons arsenal for nonnuclear deterrence and now some of those weapons would count under the treaty's limits. Another concern about the treaty is that the Russians are modernizing their arsenal and manufacturing new weapons. We are the only nuclear superpower that is neither modernizing nor capable of producing new nuclear weapons.

Either Obama was out-negotiated or he was so intent on getting the treaty signed to secure a diplomatic "win" that he didn't mind giving Russia a clear advantage.

Allowing Russia to Influence U.S. Missile Defense

Worse, the New START was crafted without a serious review of past treaty violations. A recent compliance report shows that Russia continually violated the original START. But the administration has turned a blind eye and is permitting even more lax procedures.

The Russians' intentions have been clear. Before Obama signed the treaty, they expressed a desire to make the United States more vulnerable to future attacks. While discussions about the treaty were under way, [Russian] Prime Minister Vladimir Putin commented on American missile defenses last December [2009], "By building such an umbrella over themselves, [the United States] could feel themselves fully secure and will do whatever they want." And Putin got what he wanted. After Obama signed the treaty, the Russian government issued a statement that the treaty "can operate and be viable only if the United States refrains from developing its missile defense capabilities quantitatively or qualitatively."

Russia should not be permitted to dictate whether we can develop our missile defense capabilities. No negotiations should require a sacrifice of sovereignty. The United States has a constitutional duty to protect its citizens and a moral obligation to protect its allies.

To secure his first major diplomatic victory, Obama used U.S. missile defense systems as a negotiating tool. But national security is not something to be given away.

New Policies Weaken the US Missile Defense Program

Baker Spring

Baker Spring is a research fellow in national security policy in the Allison Center for Foreign Policy Studies at the Heritage Foundation.

The Department of Defense released its Ballistic Missile Defense Review Report (BMDRR) on February 1, 2010, laying out America's long-term policy on ballistic missile defense. At the same time, the [Barack] Obama administration released its fiscal year (FY) 2011 budget request, which includes recommended funding levels for the overall ballistic missile defense program and for the portion of the program that falls under the Missile Defense Agency (MDA). The Defense Department is requesting $9.9 billion for the overall program in FY 2011, including $8.4 billion for the MDA. The remaining $1.5 billion would mainly go to the army's ballistic missile defense programs, including the Patriot interceptor and the Medium Extended Air Defense System (MEADS) program.

Treading Water

Taken together, the BMDRR and the budget clearly indicate that the ballistic missile defense program will tread water in FY 2011. The BMDRR proposes significant steps forward for some programs, such as the sea-based Aegis system and its land-based variant, particularly when compared to the programmatic retreats that the administration has imposed on other programs in FY 2010. On the other hand, these steps forward may be temporary because they are reversible. Further, the BMDRR proposes continuing retreats in other programs, such as the Airborne Laser system. On the budget side, the Obama administration's $8.4 billion request for the MDA is more than $500 million above projected spending for the current fiscal year. On the other hand, it is almost $1 billion less than the [George W.] Bush administration's budget request for the MDA for FY 2009.

A missile defense program that is simply treading water should be unacceptable to Congress because ballistic missile proliferation trends, including those described in the BMDRR, point to other countries, particularly the rogue states Iran and North Korea, developing missiles of increasing sophistication and range. Further, a program that is treading water will deprive the U.S. of the opportunity to establish improved relations with China and Russia based on more defensive strategic postures. Accordingly, Congress needs to demonstrate its commitment to both invigorating and accelerating the ballistic missile defense effort. After all, this program is about defending the U.S. and its allies against strategic attack, and the federal government has no more important responsibility under the Constitution.

The BMDRR presents the Obama administration's long-term vision for ballistic missile defense. The report contains a number of worthy observations and recommendations, but also commits several errors of commission and omission that will weaken the overall ballistic missile defense effort. The BMDRR is divided into six topic areas, each of which is worthy of examination by Congress.

Assessing Emerging Ballistic Missile Threats

The BMDRR description of the current and projected expansion of ballistic missile capabilities around the world arrives at a number of reasonable conclusions. For example, it states that both the quality and the quantity of missiles are increasing around the world. The trends point to missiles of increasing accuracy and range, use of countermeasures, and access to biological, chemical, and nuclear warheads. The BMDRR acknowledges that many states are increasing their inventories.

However, the BMDRR's assessment of the projected expansion of ballistic missile capabilities suffers from a central contradiction and several errors of omission. The report's central contradiction is that, while pointing to the increasing range of missile inventories around the world, it downplays the capabilities to attack the U.S. homeland.

In fact, justifying of the distinction between capabilities to attack the U.S. homeland and regional threats is difficult on two grounds. First, missile development programs do not pursue shorter-range and long-range missile technology independently of each other. For example, Iran has already fielded a number of different shorter-range missiles and has launched a satellite, which demonstrates an inherent capability to field longer-range missiles capable of carrying light warheads. Second, states with shorter-range missiles could pursue alternative deployment options to give them the ability to attack the U.S. homeland. The most obvious option is to place short-range missiles and launchers on cargo vessels off the U.S. coast.

Two omissions in the report are particularly important. First, the BMDRR alludes to the expansion of countermeasures to confuse or overwhelm defensive systems, but does not describe these programs in any detail. This omission makes it impossible to determine whether the ballistic missile defense policy and program outlined later in the report is responsive to countermeasure developments. Second, the BMDRR does not discuss the capability of countries to target the U.S. and its allies with electromagnetic pulse (EMP) weapons and how ballistic missiles could deliver EMP warheads. The unclassified reports of the Commission to Assess the Threat to the United States from Electromagnetic Pulse Attack clearly stated that the U.S. is quite vulnerable to this form of attack.

However, the BMDRR's most glaring omission is the lack of even a summary examination of the immediate or future indications of hostile intent toward the U.S. and its allies. A threat is the combination of capabilities and intentions. While the U.S. should urgently pursue its missile defense program because of the current and projected trends in capabilities, understanding intentions remains critically important because intentions can change with no notice.

The hostile intentions of other international actors should strongly influence how the military will operate and employ ballistic missile defense systems. However, in describing the threat, the report fails to provide even a sample of the stated hostile intentions of the leaders of several key states and non-state actors. This is not to say that these statements necessarily will result in strategic attacks on the U.S. and its allies, but they would help to prepare U.S. political leaders and the leaders of U.S. allies for the possibility of such attacks.

For example, the report does not point out that Alexander Prokhanov, a Russian writer close to the Russian General Staff, has written, "We [Russia] were not defeated by the West in the Cold War, because the Cold War continues. We lost gigantic territories, but we held Moscow. From here we launched our counterattack."

Chinese Senior Colonel Liu Mingfu reportedly stated in his book *The China Dream* that the U.S. and China are in a "competition to be the leading country, a conflict over who rises and falls to dominate the world."

In 2009, around the time of Iran's satellite launch and the 30th anniversary of the Islamic revolution, Iranian religious leader Ayatollah Ahmad Jannati stated:

The noble and prosperous Iranian nation hit another severe punch against the head of the Americans and the Israelis with that move, starting a soft enemy breaking plan against those who are planning for overthrowing the system softly. . . .

They [the United States and Israel] have to get the message and decide whether they wish to confront a 70 million strong nation and urge them to surrender, since the message of the [anniversary] rallies was that this nation will not surrender, and is faithful to Islam, the late Imam [Khomeini], and the revolution, and is still an enemy of the United States.

General Mohammad Ali Jafari, commander of the Iranian Revolutionary Guard, has stated, "Our missile capability puts all of the Zionist regime [Israel] within Iran's reach to attack."

The reality is that future hostility by Russia and/or China toward the U.S. and its allies is a distinct possibility.

After Hezbollah [an Iranian-backed terrorist group in Lebanon] launched thousands of rockets and missiles into Israel in 2006, Hezbollah spokesman Anwar Raja stated in January 2009, "Don't be surprised to see more rockets launched into northern Israel."

Regarding U.S. ally South Korea, North Korea has stated in the context of U.S.-South Korean contingency planning: "We will start a pan-national holy war of retaliation to blow away the den of South Korean authorities, including the presidential Blue House, who have led and supported the drawing up of this plan."

The North Korean state-run newspaper *Minju Joson* said in a commentary carried by the official Korean Central News Agency, "Our nuclear deterrent will be a strong defensive means . . . as well as a merciless offensive means to deal a just retaliatory strike to those who touch the country's dignity and sovereignty even a bit."

The BMDRR's failure to examine these hostile intentions permits it to downplay threats, particularly from China and Russia. The reality is that future hostility by Russia and/or China toward the U.S. and its allies is a distinct possibility, and ballistic missile defense policies and programs should address this possibility accordingly. While hostile intentions of Hezbollah, Iran, and North Korea are obvious, the BMDRR could have served a useful purpose by reminding both Congress and the American people how extreme these hostile intentions have become.

Ballistic Missile Defense Strategy and Policy

The BMDRR then proceeds to describe the Obama administration's policy for defending against the threats described in the first part of the report. This policy statement has six essential provisions:

1. A commitment to defend the U.S. homeland against limited long-range missile attacks;
2. A commitment to defend deployed U.S. forces and U.S. allies against regional missile threats;
3. The adoption of a robust testing regime;
4. The pursuit of an affordable missile defense program, which emphasizes more mature technologies over less advanced ones;
5. A hedging strategy for addressing future missile threats; and
6. Expanded international cooperation in ballistic missile defense.

As may be expected, the policy prescriptions when taken together have both good and bad aspects. On the positive side of the ledger, the administration may be starting to recognize that adopting a multilateral version of the strategic policy of mutual vulnerability that the U.S. pursued with the Soviet Union during the Cold War is problematic. Exercises conducted by the Heritage Foundation in 2005 demonstrated that the absence of defenses in a setting of proliferation of both nuclear weapons and ballistic missile delivery systems is highly destabilizing and carries a relatively high risk of the use of nuclear weapons.

Second, the BMDRR acknowledges that ballistic missile defense's essential roles are bolstering deterrence, maintaining the policy of extending deterrence to U.S. allies, and reassuring U.S. allies about the threats that they face. This is a welcome departure from the Cold War assertion that missile defenses are destabilizing and incompatible with deterrence. Finally, the report indicates that the administration accepts in principle the wisdom of pursuing options with both China and Russia to establish more defensive strategic postures by helping both to "better understand the stabilizing benefits of missile defense."

On the negative side of the ledger, the BMDRR's policy prescriptions include steps that contradict or undermine the positive elements. First, it states that missile defenses to protect the U.S. homeland are being limited, at least relative to regional defenses. This is to preserve, at least for the near term, the policy of mutual vulnerability toward both China and Russia. Continuing this policy of vulnerability toward China and Russia undermines to a considerable degree the recognition that missile defenses play positive roles in extended deterrence and reassurance to U.S. allies. The report apparently assumes that the defense of U.S. allies against regional missile threats is sufficient and that direct threats against the U.S. will not weaken the security links to U.S. allies. However, direct threats to the U.S. will weaken these links.

Second, the missile defense policy recommended in the BMDRR displays a bias in development policy toward near-term capabilities at the expense of forward-looking technological developments. For example, no statement in the policy shows that the administration understands that the most effective defense against ballistic missiles for both the U.S. and its allies is a network of space-based interceptors.

Finally, there is one glaring omission in the BMDRR's policy provisions: arms control. Arms control is clearly the

Obama administration's most important foreign policy priority; the report does not discuss how missile defense fits into the administration's overall arms control agenda. This may indicate that the Obama administration has something to hide. During the campaign, President Obama made an unequivocal and unqualified commitment not to "weaponize" space, despite the fact that space is already weaponized.

In 2009, the administration entered into negotiations at the Conference on Disarmament on the subject of preventing an arms race in outer space. An international agreement on this subject will almost certainly require the administration to dismantle the vast majority of the missile defense programs that it claims to support in the BMDRR. For example, all of the versions of the Standard Missile-3 (SM-3) that the administration says that it wants to pursue under its missile defense program will have an inherent anti-satellite capability. They will need to be severely curtailed, if not banned outright, under a space weapons agreement. President Obama's nomination of Philip Coyle to the position of associate director for national security and international affairs in the Office of Science and Technology Policy is currently on hold because the nominee failed to answer a question about the possible defense systems and programs that could be defined as having a direct or contributory capability as anti-satellite weapons.

Defending the Homeland

The BMDRR makes it clear that the Obama administration intends to stand by its 2009 decision to retreat on the fielding of the Ground-Based Midcourse Defense (GMD) system to defend the U.S. and Europe against long-range missiles. The Bush administration planned to field 54 interceptors: 44 in Alaska and California and 10 in Poland. The Obama administration is planning to field just 30 interceptors, with none in Poland.

The BMDRR asserts that the Obama administration is "hedging" against uncertainties about future ballistic missile threats to the U.S. homeland. If the administration had a serious program for hedging against these uncertainties, the report would include additional steps, including:

1. Fielding the total number of GMD interceptors proposed by the Bush administration;

2. Accelerated fielding of the SM-3 Block IIB, which will have a capability to counter long-range missiles;

3. Continuing the momentum behind the Airborne Laser program, not relegating it to a technology demonstration program;

4. Maintaining missile defense options to counter the threat from short-range missiles launched off the U.S. coast; and

5. Most importantly, developing and fielding a constellation of space-based interceptors based on the Brilliant Pebbles technology developed during the [Ronald] Reagan and George H. W. Bush administrations.

The United States needs to address the unique security challenges posed by the post–Cold War world, and a robust missile defense program is essential.

Defending Against Regional Threats

In contrast to the Obama administration's retreats in other areas of ballistic missile defense, the BMDRR indicates that the administration plans to continue to advance the Bush administration programs for countering short-range, medium-range, and intermediate-range missiles. The "phased adaptive approach" is focused on advancing the currently sea-based Aegis missile defense system and its SM-3 interceptors.

The overall approach envisions a four-step program:

1. Between now and FY 2011, procure more of the existing system.

2. Around 2015, develop more advanced versions of the SM-3 (the SM-3 Block IB) to provide broader coverage and deploy them on land. The initial emphasis will be to deploy these interceptors in southern Europe.

3. Around 2018, field SM-3 Block IIA interceptors, which are already under development, primarily to counter medium-range and intermediate-range missiles. This would include fielding interceptors in northern Europe to protect U.S. NATO [North Atlantic Treaty Organization] allies in Europe.

4. Around 2020, deploy SM-3 Block IIB interceptors to counter long-range ballistic missiles that could threaten the U.S. homeland as well as regional allies.

The phased adaptive approach for improving the Aegis system and the SM-3 interceptors can succeed, but success depends on the Obama administration providing sustained funding to the program. It also requires that neither the administration nor Congress impede progress by placing policy-related or programmatic barriers in the way. The most likely policy-related barriers would stem from arms control, including buckling to Russian demands to curtail the missile defense program in negotiations on the Strategic Arms Reduction Treaty (START) follow-on treaty or in pursuing agreements on space arms. The most likely programmatic barriers are attempts to impose traditional acquisition rules on the systems and allowing the MDA, which traditionally has opposed the Aegis-based missile defense system, to lay out a program for advancing Aegis and SM-3 technology, but the program remains reversible. . . .

A Robust Missile Defense Needed

In 2009, the Obama administration set back the missile defense program by cutting the funding for the program and by terminating or curtailing certain elements of it. It has repeated that approach in its proposal for FY 2011 and beyond. The question for Congress is whether the Obama administration's BMDRR and proposed FY 2011 missile defense budget signal a permanent course change on missile defense or only a momentary pause before the administration resumes its effort to weaken the missile defense program.

There may be no direct answer to this question because the Obama administration may be divided internally on this matter. This makes it even more important for Congress to state unequivocally that it supports a robust missile defense program to protect the American people, U.S. forces in the field, and U.S. friends and allies. The United States needs to address the unique security challenges posed by the post–Cold War world, and a robust missile defense program is essential to meeting these challenges effectively. Congress can make sure the Obama administration makes the right decision on missile defense.

New Missile Defense Policies Are Sound

Michael O'Hanlon

Michael O'Hanlon is director of research and a senior fellow at the Brookings Institution, a public policy organization based in Washington, D.C.

Last week [September 2009], the [Barack] Obama administration announced that it was canceling plans for the missile-defense network in Europe first proposed by the [George W.] Bush administration in 2007. The program would have deployed a radar system in the Czech Republic linked to other radar stations on the continent and a base of ten interceptor missiles in Poland. Its purpose was to shield western Europe and the United States from medium- and long-range missiles launched from Iran.

In the days since the decision was announced, a number of critics have suggested that the move reflects the new administration's lack of seriousness about the missile threat and perhaps a worrisome proclivity to try to please Russia, which had protested against the planned architecture.

This is not the first time the Obama administration has come under fire for its approach to missile defense. Last spring, Secretary of Defense Robert Gates reduced funding for the program by about $2 billion a year, leading some conservatives to argue that the United States was sending the wrong message to countries with potentially adversarial missile programs such as China, Iran, and North Korea.

Maintaining U.S. Missile Defenses

As I first described in *Foreign Affairs* ten years ago, the debate over missile defense is often mired in ideology more than it is grounded in real fact. Today is no different—and ultimately, the criticism over the Obama administration's latest move is not compelling. Take the budget for missile-defense programs: After reaching $12 billion a year during the Bush administration, the U.S. military now spends about $10 billion annually. Although some may see this figure as a sign of the United States' declining resolve to counter offensive-missile threats, it is 50 percent greater than what Ronald Reagan devoted to missile defense under the Strategic Defense Initiative, more popularly known as "Star Wars."

It is hard, therefore, to view President Barack Obama's cutback as seriously lessening the United States' commitment to the long-term goal of defending itself and its allies from missile attack. As a combined system, missile defense remains one of the Pentagon's largest acquisition programs in size and cost. Moreover, the recent budgetary cuts are not distributed carelessly across all programs—while some suffered, others were sustained and even expanded.

It is likely that the missile-defense system based in the Czech Republic and Poland would have worked—at least against a small and simple attack without a large number of warheads or decoys. The plan relied on technology similar to that already deployed in Alaska and California, whose systems are designed to protect against a possible launch from North Korea. Although not trivial, the expected cost of the program—around $6 billion over the next decade or so—was not huge. But it would have taken several years to come to fruition and would have protected western Europe against only the first half dozen missiles in any future attack, not to mention leaving parts of southern Europe entirely unprotected.

The Czech-Polish proposal, however, was not the only missile-defense program Obama inherited when he entered office. The Pentagon has several ideas in various states of development, production, and deployment: the Patriot missile (for a ground-based defense against missiles in the final or "terminal" stage of flight); Terminal High Altitude Area Defense, a ground-based defense against mid-flight threats of modest range; the system in Alaska and California, a ground-based defense against long-range missile threats; the U.S. Navy's Aegis/Standard missile system against missile threats over or near the sea; and the airborne laser and the kinetic-energy interceptor, which are designed to work against missiles in their boost phase just after launch.

With last week's decision, the backbone of U.S. missile defense in Europe appears to have shifted to the Standard Missile-3 (SM-3), a ship-based antiballistic missile that can also be adapted to sites on land. The Obama administration's strategy for announcing the change was suboptimal, as it failed to anticipate some of the criticisms and concerns on both sides of the Atlantic and buried much of the technical detail for the program in its releases online and in the media. Administration officials have made some useful correctives, however: Gates suggested that SM-3 missiles could someday be deployed in the Czech Republic and Poland, and Secretary of State Hillary Clinton made a resolute commitment to sustain alliances with both countries in comments at the Brookings Institution last week.

Foreign Relations Concerns

NATO [North Atlantic Treaty Organization] politics are another concern. Many NATO members support the general idea of a missile-defense system, yet they wonder why Washington originally decided to pursue the issue primarily as a two-track process with the Czech Republic and Poland—two new, modestly sized members of the alliance—given the strategic implications for NATO as a whole. Wisely, the new approach appears to have involved the United States' NATO allies more fully.

It is worth emphasizing that Russia's objections to the Czech and Polish sites were without strategic merit. Russia has several thousand ballistic missiles; in the unthinkable event of a nuclear war between it and the West, the United States' defense system in central Europe would be like using a flyswatter against a bazooka. Furthermore, Russia has the technology to deploy the kind of countermeasures that would render a relatively small defense system entirely useless. Russia, therefore, should receive no special treatment for its behavior, and NATO should avoid making any long-term commitments about the future of missile defense in central Europe.

That said, for a new administration seeking to "reset" relations with Moscow, it makes sense, at least for now, to avoid what had become a major strain in U.S.-Russian relations. Although much of the blame for escalating the missile-defense dispute lies with Russia, the United States has contributed, too. Last year, during the height of Russia's crisis with Georgia, Dana Perino, the Bush administration's press secretary, said that the United States' decision to formalize the missile-defense plan with Warsaw and Prague was "mostly coincidental." She, along with others inside the U.S. government, thus gave some credence to Russia's otherwise baseless fear that the system was designed against its interests.

It is doubtful that Obama's cancellation of this program will immediately inspire much help from Moscow on Tehran's nuclear program or any other policy issue. But even a modest improvement is nothing to sneeze at, provided that the United States sends a clear message to Moscow not to threaten or bully new NATO members in the future.

There is one problem with the Obama administration's missile-defense policies, however: boost-phase systems are no longer being seriously developed. Such systems act early in an enemy missile's flight, depriving that missile of the chance to deploy decoys that can fool many systems—such as the U.S. sites in Alaska and California, the SM-3, and the proposed

Czech-and-Polish system. In April, Gates canceled both of the United States' two main boost-phase programs: the airborne laser and the kinetic-energy interceptor. Critics of the Obama administration's missile-defense policies should focus their concerns on this set of decisions. It may, for example, make sense to purchase more than just the one airborne laser system that is being retained as a test platform, even if the original plan to buy 20 was too much.

On balance, though, the Obama administration is making sound and solid decisions on missile defense. It is robustly funding and deploying the kinds of systems that are most responsive to the threats the United States is facing now and is likely to face in the near future.

Organizations to Contact

The editors have compiled the following list of organizations concerned with the issues debated in this book. The descriptions are derived from materials provided by the organizations. All have publications or information available for interested readers. The list was compiled on the date of publication of the present volume; the information provided here may change. Be aware that many organizations take several weeks or longer to respond to inquiries, so allow as much time as possible.

Beyond Nuclear

6930 Carroll Avenue, Suite 400, Takoma Park, MD   20912
(301) 270-2209 • fax: (301) 270-4000
e-mail: info@beyondnuclear.org
website: www.beyondnuclear.org

Beyond Nuclear is an advocacy organization that seeks the elimination of all nuclear weapons and argues that removing such weapons can only make us safer, not more vulnerable. The Beyond Nuclear team works with diverse partners and allies to provide the public, government officials, and the media with information about the dangers of nuclear weapons and nuclear power. The group's website offers publications such as fact sheets, reports, press releases, congressional testimony, articles, and videos.

Bulletin of the Atomic Scientists

1155 E. Sixtieth Street, Chicago, IL   60637
(773) 382-8057
e-mail: kbenedict@thebulletin.org
website: www.thebulletin.org

The Bulletin of the Atomic Scientists was established in 1945 by scientists, engineers, and other experts who had created the atomic bomb as part of the US Manhattan Project. The group informs the public about threats to the survival and development of humanity from nuclear weapons, climate change, and emerging technologies in the life sciences. It publishes a magazine, also called the *Bulletin of the Atomic Scientists*, and maintains a feature called the Doomsday Clock, which conveys how close humanity is to nuclear and other types of catastrophic destruction—the figurative midnight and new developments in the life sciences that could inflict irrevocable harm. The current *Bulletin* and past issues are available on the group's website.

Carnegie Endowment for International Peace

1779 Massachusetts Avenue NW
Washington, DC 20036-2103
(202) 483-7600 • fax: (202) 483-1840
e-mail: info@carnegieendowment.org
website: www.carnegieendowment.org

The Carnegie Endowment for International Peace is a private, nonprofit organization dedicated to advancing cooperation between nations and promoting active international engagement by the United States. It publishes *Foreign Policy*, a magazine of global politics, economics, and ideas, and a search of the group's website produces numerous publications about nuclear weapons. Two examples include "Abolishing Nuclear Weapons: A Debate" and "Abolishing Nuclear Weapons: Why the United States Should Lead."

Center for International Security and Cooperation (CISAC)

Freeman Spogli Institute for International Studies
Stanford, CA 94305-6055
(650) 723-9625 • fax: (650) 725-2592
website: http://cisac.stanford.edu

The Center for International Security and Cooperation (CISAC), part of the Freeman Spogli Institute for International Studies (FSI), is an interdisciplinary, university-based research and training center that addresses some of the world's most difficult security problems with policy-relevant solutions. The center is committed to scholarly research and to giving independent advice to governments and international organizations. CISAC seeks international security through cooperation among peoples and governments. The CISAC website is a source of scholarly research in many forms, including working papers circulated among subject experts, reports and policy briefings presented at meetings, and the more formal peer-reviewed writings of journals and books. Two 2010 examples of its publications include "India and the NPT" and "U.S. Policy Toward the Korean Peninsula."

Heritage Foundation

214 Massachusetts Avenue NE, Washington, DC   20002-4999
(202) 546-4400
website: www.heritage.org

Founded in 1973, the Heritage Foundation is a research and educational institution—a think tank—whose mission is to formulate and promote conservative public policies based on the principles of free enterprise, limited government, individual freedom, traditional American values, and a strong national defense. Among the issues that concern the foundation are nuclear arms control and proliferation, missile defense, and national security and defense. Recent publications relevant to nuclear armament include "Strategic Nuclear Arms Control for the Protect and Defend Strategy" and "Nuclear Games: An Exercise Examining Stability and Defenses in a Proliferated World."

International Physicians for the Prevention of Nuclear War (IPPNW)

66-70 Union Square, #204, Somerville, MA   02143
(617) 440-1733 • fax: (617) 440-1734
e-mail: ippnwbos@ippnw.org
website: www.ippnw.org

International Physicians for the Prevention of Nuclear War (IPPNW) is a nonpartisan federation of national medical organizations in sixty-two countries, representing thousands of doctors, medical students, health workers, and concerned citizens who share the goal of creating a more peaceful and secure world freed from the threat of nuclear annihilation. IPPNW is committed to ending war and advancing understanding of the causes of armed conflict from a public health perspective. The group's website contains links to numerous books and publications, fact sheets, and periodicals on the subject of nuclear armament.

James Martin Center for Nonproliferation Studies (CNS)
460 Pierce Street, Monterey, CA   93940
(831) 647-4154 • fax: (831) 647-3519
e-mail: cns@miis.edu
website: http://cns.miis.edu

The James Martin Center for Nonproliferation Studies (CNS) is the largest nongovernmental organization in the world devoted to curbing the spread of weapons of mass destruction, and it is the only organization dedicated exclusively to graduate education and research on nonproliferation issues. CNS writes and distributes a number of ongoing publications, including the *Nonproliferation Review*, a journal concerned with the causes, consequences, and control of the spread of nuclear, chemical, biological, and conventional weapons, and the *Inventory of International Nonproliferation Organizations and Regimes*, a reference book of international organizations, treaties, and agreements relevant to nuclear disarmament and nonproliferation activities. The CNS website also provides various papers on nuclear weapons issues.

Union of Concerned Scientists (UCS)
Two Brattle Square, Cambridge, MA   02138-3780
(617) 547-5552 • fax: (617) 864-9405
website: www.ucsusa.org

The Union of Concerned Scientists (UCS) was founded in 1969 by a group of scientists and students at the Massachusetts Institute of Technology to protest the militarization of scientific research and promote science in the public interest.

Since its founding, UCS has focused on nuclear weapons and nuclear power, and it works to eliminate the risks posed by nuclear weapons, nuclear terrorism, and space weapons. The UCS website is a good source of information about nuclear armament. Recent UCS publications include "All Things Nuclear—Insights on Science and Security" and "Key Elements of the FY 2011 Budget Request for Nuclear Weapons and Nonproliferation."

Bibliography

Books

Jeremy Bernstein — *Nuclear Weapons: What You Need to Know.* New York: Cambridge University Press, 2008.

Michael E. Brown et al., eds. — *Going Nuclear: Nuclear Proliferation and International Security in the 21st Century.* Cambridge, MA: MIT Press, 2010.

Joseph Cirincione — *Bomb Scare: The History and Future of Nuclear Weapons.* New York: Columbia University Press, 2007.

Stephanie Cooke — *In Mortal Hands: A Cautionary History of the Nuclear Age.* New York: Bloomsbury, 2009.

Brian Michael Jenkins — *Will Terrorists Go Nuclear?* Amherst, NY: Prometheus Books, 2008.

Michael Levi — *On Nuclear Terrorism.* Cambridge, MA: Harvard University Press, 2007.

Sverre Lodgaard — *Nuclear Disarmament and Non-Proliferation: Towards a Nuclear-Weapon Free World?* New York: Routledge, 2010.

Jerry Miller — *Stockpile: The Story Behind 10,000 Strategic Nuclear Weapons.* Annapolis, MD: Naval Institute Press, 2010.

John Mueller — *Atomic Obsession: Nuclear Alarmism from Hiroshima to Al Qaeda*. New York: Oxford University Press, 2010.

Norman Polmar and Robert S. Norris — *The U.S. Nuclear Arsenal: A History of Weapons and Delivery Systems Since 1945*. Annapolis, MD: Naval Institute Press, 2009.

Michael Quinlan — *Thinking About Nuclear Weapons: Principles, Problems, Prospects*. New York: Oxford University Press, 2009.

Thomas C. Reed and Danny B. Stillman — *The Nuclear Express: A Political History of the Bomb and Its Proliferation*. Minneapolis, MN: Zenith Press, 2009.

Richard Rhodes — *The Twilight of the Bombs: Recent Challenges, New Dangers, and the Prospects for a World Without Nuclear Weapons*. New York: Alfred A. Knopf, 2010.

Joseph M. Siracusa — *Nuclear Weapons: A Very Short Introduction*. New York: Oxford University Press, 2008.

Stephen M. Younger — *The Bomb: A New History*. New York: Ecco Press, 2009.

Periodicals and Internet Sources

Turner Brinton — "GOP Pledges to Fully Fund Missile Defense," *Space News*, September 27, 2010. http://spacenews.com.

Peter Brookes   "Troubling START Treaty Gives
                      Russia Too Much," *Real Clear Politics*,
                      May 15, 2010.
                      www.realclearpolitics.com.

Adrian Brune   "The Great Nuclear Race in South
                      Asia," *Foreign Policy Digest*, July 1,
                      2010. www.foreignpolicydigest.org.

Ivan Eland   "Will Eliminating Nuclear Weapons
                      Make Peace More Likely?"
                      Antiwar.com, March 3, 2010.
                      http://original.antiwar.com.

Robert Farley   "Why Did the Nuclear Posture
                      Review Bomb?" *American Prospect*,
                      April 8, 2010. www.prospect.org.

Nazila Fathi and   "Decrying U.S., Iran Begins War
David E. Sanger   Games," *New York Times*, April 21,
                      2010. www.nytimes.com.

Fissile Materials   "Preventing Nuclear Terrorism,"
Working Group   *Bulletin of the Atomic Scientists*,
                      March 30, 2010. www.thebulletin.org.

Sumit Ganguly   "A Dangerous Place," *Newsweek*, May
                      8, 2008. www.newsweek.com.

Jacob Heilbrunn   "The New START Treaty Deserves to
                      Be Ratified," *Los Angeles Times*, July
                      12, 2010. http://articles.latimes.com.

Robert Jervis   "Or: How I Learned to Stop
                      Worrying," *National Interest*, October
                      27, 2009. http://nationalinterest.org.

Alex Kingsbury "A Change for U.S. Nuclear Strategy," *U.S. News & World Report*, April 13, 2010. http://politics.usnews.com.

Michael Levi "Stopping Nuclear Terrorism: The Dangerous Allure of a Perfect Defense," *Foreign Affairs*, January–February 2008. www.foreignaffairs.com.

Robert Marquand "Nuclear Weapons: Is Full Disarmament Possible?" *Christian Science Monitor*, April 6, 2010. www.csmonitor.com.

Greg Mitchell "How the First Nuclear Blast, 65 Years Ago Today, Set Truman on Path to Hiroshima," *Huffington Post*, July 16, 2010. www.huffingtonpost.com.

New York Post "Hiroshima: No Apology Needed," August 6, 2010. www.nypost.com.

Sam Nunn, Igor Ivanov, Wolfgang Ischinger "All Together Now: Missile Defense," *New York Times*, July 21, 2010. www.nytimes.com.

Steven Pifer and Strobe Talbott "Judging the New START Treaty," *Politico*, March 29, 2010. www.politico.com.

Luv Puri "Getting Real About Nuclear Terrorism," Dawn.com, February 2, 2010. http://blog.dawn.com.

Baker Spring — "The Nuclear Posture Review's Missing Objective: Defending the U.S. and Its Allies Against Strategic Attack," Heritage Foundation, April 14, 2010. www.heritage.org.

Jonathan Tepperman — "Why Obama Should Learn to Love the Bomb," *Newsweek*, August 29, 2009. www.newsweek.com.

Richard Weitz — "Counterpoint: On Missile Defense," *New York Times*, July 23, 2010. www.nytimes.com.

Micah Zenko and Michael Levi — "Three Steps to Reducing Nuclear Terrorism," *Christian Science Monitor*, January 25, 2010. www.csmonitor.com.

Index

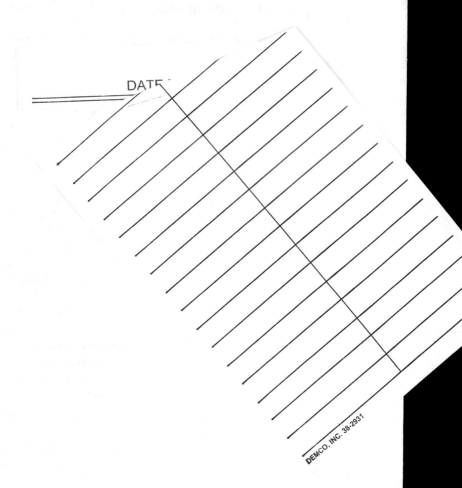

DATE

DEMCO, INC. 38-2931